"Essential reading for the novice and the veter steers thought, stirs emotion, and spurs actic
—**Abraham Kuruvilla**, Senior Researcl.
Pastoral Ministries, Dallas Theologicaɹ ᴜ

"All of us who preach have regretted some of the sermons we delivered early in our ministries. And all of us who teach preaching have done the same with some of our first lectures and classroom exercises. How I wish I would have had access to a resource like *Training Preachers* before I walked into my first seminary classroom as a professor! While there's a plethora of books available to preachers and students of preaching, few have been written on the slippery subject of how to teach things related to this holy calling. Whether you're just starting out or you're a seasoned preaching coach, Scott Gibson and his team of experienced homileticians have provided us with a treasure for our task."
—**Jim Shaddix**, W. A. Criswell Professor of Expository Preaching
and Director, Center for Preaching and Pastoral Leadership,
Southeastern Baptist Theological Seminary

"Over the course of the last twenty years, more than thirteen hundred books have been published on the subject of preaching. Few of these works are specifically designed to resource homiletics teachers for the task of instructing preachers. *Training Preachers* astutely fills this void to the greater glory of God and the greater good of the church. As a treasure chest of education-based guidance for teaching preaching, *Training Preachers* is a rare find--a gem. Readers will discover a goldmine of sound principles and proven practices for effectively equipping learners in the art and science of life-changing proclamation."
—**France B. Brown, Jr.**, Dr. Ernest L. Mays Assistant Professor of
Expository Preaching & Biblical Teaching,
College of Biblical Studies–Houston

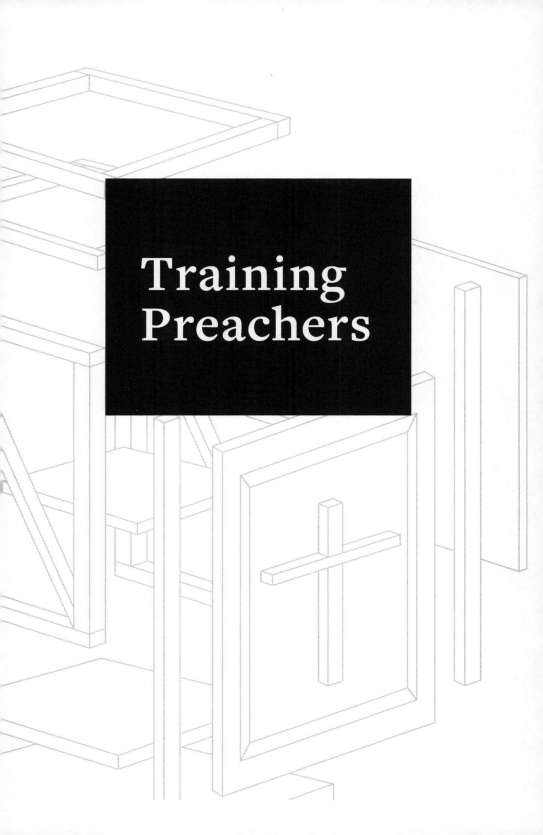

Training
Preachers

Training Preachers

A Guide to Teaching Homiletics

Edited by
Scott M. Gibson

LEXHAM PRESS

Training Preachers: A Guide to Teaching Homiletics

Copyright 2018 Scott M. Gibson

Lexham Press, 1313 Commercial St., Bellingham, WA 98225
LexhamPress.com

Print ISBN 9781683592068
Digital ISBN 9781683592075

Lexham Editorial Team: Jim Weaver, Elliot Ritzema, Karen Engle
Cover Design: George Siler
Interior Design: Nicholas Richardson

24 vii / US

In honor of Bruce and Joan Aiken
Faithful sermon listeners and faithful followers of Christ

Contents

o o o

Preface

SCOTT M. GIBSON

This project grew out of a concern for teachers of preaching to have instruction in educational theory to help them become better at what they do. My own undergraduate degree in education has enabled me to apply educational theory and practice to my classes for more than twenty-five years. Often, I give thanks for my training in education. It has helped me immensely in the planning of classes, execution of exercises, and assessment of student work.

In 2014, the Lilly Endowment invited the Haddon W. Robinson Center for Preaching at Gordon-Conwell Theological Seminary to participate in a five-year grant (2015–2019) called the Initiative to Strengthen Christian Preaching. Along with seventeen other theological institutions, we began to explore how we might, in our context, strengthen Christian preaching.

One of the requests from Lilly was that grantees focus on some aspect of andragogy/pedagogy—the teaching of preaching. At Gordon-Conwell we could have evaluated the preaching curriculum, or we might have conducted a survey that students would complete before they enrolled in preaching courses and then after they studied preaching to determine development of homiletical skills, or any other study. Instead, we lifted our gaze more broadly. My hope was to see out of this a larger and wider impact on the field of homiletics, concentrating on the teaching of preaching. By tackling the andragogy/pedagogy of the teaching of preaching, we would be able to influence the education of present and future professors of preaching and, hopefully, have an impact on the generations of professors and students yet to come.

Our plan was to bring together professors of preaching who themselves have either an undergraduate or graduate degree in education. We would meet for a day to discuss the needs in the teaching of preaching and then decide what to do.

At the one-day consultation, we outlined a book that would provide the contours of educational theory and practice that a first-year preaching professor would need to begin teaching. Invitees to the consultation were assigned chapters to write. After the chapters were written, we convened another consultation to discuss what we learned from writing our own chapter and from each other's chapters. The day was rich with learning— and even suggested other possible writing projects to address additional matters in the teaching of preaching.

A book like this does not come to be by itself. I want to first express my appreciation to Dr. John Wimmer, program director, religion, at The Lilly Endowment, Inc. I am grateful for your continued support and interest in the place of preaching in theological education and the church.

Thank you also to the authors who contributed to this book. Your insights in the consultation gatherings and the resulting chapters will only bolster the task of teaching preachers to preach. Well done!

Thanks a million to Jim Weaver. Thank you for your constant investment in preaching, Jim. And thanks for believing in this project. Thanks also to Elliot Ritzema whose careful editorial shepherding of this project has shaped it into a stronger book. Thanks to my graduate assistant, Chase Jensen, who created the index. And thanks to Brannon Ellis and the rest of the team at Lexham Press for their devotion to preaching and to strengthening the Lord's people through solid publications.

Thanks to the Haddon W. Robinson Center for Preaching team who over the last few years have helped to make this book a reality. Thanks to Joe Kim, Dr. Young Kim, Ben Kim, Angus Courtney, and Josiah Cheng. Thanks also to the Ockenga team: David Currie, Bridget Erickson, Susanne McCarron, and Dorothy Guild, who assisted with the consultation arrangements and other administrative details. Thanks, too, to David Horn and Saemi Kim for your part in making this project a reality.

Thanks to Preston Conger, who assisted with the research for my chapter—well done, Preston. And thanks to Jim Darlack and the folks at the Goddard Library, Gordon-Conwell Theological Seminary.

Thanks to Alyssa J. Walker for her immense help with the project grant. Your wisdom, insight, and interest in what we're doing are greatly appreciated. Thanks, too, to Gregg Hansen who keeps the numbers straight.

Thank you, Gordon-Conwell Trustees and Administration (Drs. Hollinger and Lints) and the FPPC, for the sabbatical leave to work on projects like this!

Thank you to my former colleagues in the preaching department: Jeffrey D. Arthurs, Patricia M. Batten, Pablo Jimenez, and Matthew D. Kim. And thanks to my new colleagues at Baylor University's Truett Seminary for their commitment to the teaching of preaching.

Finally, thank you to Rhonda, my wife, for your constant support in all in which I'm involved. She dutifully listens to my sermons—and bad jokes. She carefully reads what I've written and offers helpful and insightful advice. She is constantly present, a ready, amazing model and partner in ministry. Thank you, my dear, for your sacrificial love, which reflects the Savior we serve.

This book is dedicated to my in-laws—or, as Haddon Robinson said at our wedding, "in-loves"—Bruce and Joan Aiken. They are the kind of people the preachers we educate preach to week after week. Their faith and dedication to Christ is instructive and inspiring. I'm grateful to God for them and for being part of their family. Thanks, Mom and Dad Aiken, for sharing life, love, and especially your daughter, Rhonda, with me.

○ ○ ○

Introduction to the Teaching of Preaching

SCOTT M. GIBSON

There are as many methods of teaching homiletics as
there are teachers of homiletics, and there are as many
methods of preparing sermons as there are preachers.[1]

Professors of preaching, like many of the teachers who taught them in college or university, typically do not have a philosophical or theoretical framework for doing what they do. They teach like they have been taught. They experiment. They try this technique or that tip on lecturing or student engagement, and maybe read a book on teaching. For most professors, teaching is more of a journey of discovering what works and what does not.

One preaching professor surveyed for the purposes of this book noted that he would have liked to know more about educational theory and even homiletics when he first started teaching. "In the providence of God," he wrote, "this deficiency in my training and reading cast me back on the Lord, his word, and his Spirit, which isn't a bad place to land." Nevertheless, some foundation in educational andragogy/pedagogy would have been of immense help when he first started teaching.

Once appointed, the newly minted preaching professor jumps into the flow of the academic year with the mandate to teach a certain number of courses, construct the syllabi, and make plans as to how each teaching session will flow. Yet there are other concerns that confront the fledgling teacher. "When I first started teaching," says a preaching professor, "I wish I knew that my success as a professor was not based on whether or not students liked me or grew to like preaching, but rather it was centered on

---

1. H. C. Brown Jr., ed., *Southern Baptist Preaching* (Nashville: Broadman, 1959), 3.

1

getting students to stretch themselves, grow, and learn something new about both themselves and communicating God's word."

One seasoned preaching professor contemplated, "If I were starting out again, knowing what I know now, I might say, 'Simplify the process and don't assume too much about the student's capacity. Learning how to preach is best learned through guided practice. Lecture less and mentor more. Students learn best by your response to their practice'."

THE PURPOSE OF THIS BOOK

This book was developed to help a first-year preaching professor get started. If you do not have a background in educational theory, this book is for you. The intention is to help you get a handle on what it means to *teach* preaching. You cannot do it well without the right tools, and what you will find here may help you avoid the constant experimentation in which you might otherwise have to engage.

As you begin reading, you may be thinking, "I wish I knew how to write clear objectives," or "I wish I knew more about how my students learned." If that is the case, this book is for you.

It begins in chapter 1 with an overview of the key role the professor of preaching and the teaching of preaching has played in the development of theological education in the United States, setting up a historical framework for the teaching we do. From Patricia Batten (chapter 2), Victor Anderson (chapter 3), and John Tornfelt (chapter 4) comes a focus on educational theory and the task of teaching. Two practical chapters on what a new preaching professor should expect when starting a teaching position are written by Tony Merida (chapter 5) and Blake Newsom (chapter 6). The next two chapters by Sid Buzzell (chapters 7 and 8) discuss the construction of a syllabus and the place of learning objectives in teaching. Since preaching involves student practice and feedback, Chris Rappazini (chapter 9) provides a discussion on the value of offering helpful feedback to student preachers. Finally, Timothy Bushfield (chapter 10) underscores the place of continual education personally and professionally for the preacher.

All the contributors to this book are experienced pastors/preachers and seminary teachers. Additionally, they possess either an undergraduate or graduate degree in education. In short, they understand both teaching and preaching.

FINAL WORDS

In the development of this book a survey was sent to teachers of preaching asking for responses to the following question: What do you wish you knew when you first started teaching preaching? The responses varied from educational theory to practical classroom management. One professor noted, "I had to teach and research the field of preaching during a hectic first year of developing syllabi and teaching preaching (with some administrative duties as well). I wish that I had joined a professional society while serving as a pastor." Strengthening one's foundation in educational theory and practice is further developed by becoming a part of a professional society, like the Evangelical Homiletics Society, a guild of teachers of preaching.[2]

Another professor humbly wrote, "I wish I knew that it was okay that I didn't know everything." You do not need to know everything. You can't. However, this book is intended to address some of the unanswered education-related questions and deficiencies a beginning preaching professor might have. The book does not address everything—but we hope, nevertheless, that it will be a helpful tool to those who want to strengthen their educational foundation in their teaching of homiletics.

Our goal is that you, the beginning teacher of preaching, might someday look back at your time in the classroom and say what a veteran professor of preaching said in his survey response:

> I have found my three-plus decades of teaching preaching to be deeply rewarding for at least these reasons: I have a front-row seat to witness the Holy Spirit's work of raising up the next generation for the ministry of the word; I am regularly inspired by the convictions and devotion of those training for ministry in an increasingly secular age; and, I have the privilege of contributing a small part to the preparation of those whose ministries will reverberate in the eternal lives of many. No teacher can make a "great" preacher— only the Holy Spirit has that power. But those who teach faithfully can guide conscientious students into faithful ministries that will greatly bless God's people.

---

2. See http://ehomiletics.com.

Draw direction, wisdom, and guidance from this book that will aid you in your teaching of preaching. May it help you guide your students to be faithful in the ministries God has given them so that through them they might bless, grow, and mature God's people, to the glory of God: Father, Son, and Holy Spirit.

1

o o o

The Place of Preaching Professors in Theological Education

SCOTT M. GIBSON

> *Theological schools are ideal settings for teaching, and
> the Christian tradition is a teaching tradition.*[1]

The teaching of preaching has been part of the landscape of theological education since the establishment of formal theological training in North America. In this chapter, I will show that homiletics has its forebears in tributaries from various forms of practice, yet all underscore the important place of homiletics instruction.

This chapter focuses on the developing historical position of homiletics in the framework of theological instruction, which I will address first. Then, I will explore the contours of what the training of preachers has looked like from the past to the present. Next, I will focus on the education of teachers—the education of teachers of preaching. As a result of this study, I will list some challenges facing the present field of homiletics and what the implications might be for the future, as well as provide some suggestions for addressing the challenges.

---

1. Daniel O. Aleshire, *Earthen Vessels: Hopeful Reflections on the Work and Future of Theological Schools* (Grand Rapids: Eerdmans, 2008), 23.

THE PLACE OF PREACHING IN AMERICAN
THEOLOGICAL EDUCATION

SURVEY OF HOMILETICS IN SEMINARIES

Harvard College was founded in 1636, not only to prepare ministers for the burgeoning Puritan colonies but also to prepare students in leadership for the various aspects of colonial society.[2] By 1805, the Harvard faculty was persuaded to embrace Unitarianism and voted to appoint Henry Ware, a self-proclaimed Unitarian, to the Hollis Professorship of Divinity. This led some to break with Harvard and found Andover Seminary in 1808, which was based on orthodox Trinitarian theology.[3]

What is striking about the founding of institutions like Andover and other seminaries that followed is the primacy of preaching in the theological curriculum. Unlike the British universities like Oxford or Cambridge where clergy were trained and where preaching was not part of the curriculum, their American counterpart theological schools placed preaching in the forefront, moving it into a distinct academic discipline.

Even in Britain, however, there were notable exceptions to the prevailing model. Philip Doddridge, for example, led an academy where practical studies like preaching were taught to every theological student.[4] Additionally, continental theologians like J. J. Van Oosterzee advocated for the "idea and importance of homiletics."[5] Van Oosterzee demonstrated high regard for homiletics in the theological curriculum, its place as a distinct discipline. He urged:

> Christian Homiletics is that part of Practical Theology which describes the nature of and requirements for the preaching of the Gospel in the congregational assemblies of the Christian Church, with the definite object of training by this method well-qualified

---

2. Harry S. Stout, *The New England Soul: Preaching and Religious Culture in Colonial New England* (New York: Oxford University Press, 1986), 89.

3. *General Catalogue of the Theological Seminary, Andover, Massachusetts, 1808–1908* (Boston: Thomas Todd, 1909), ii.

4. Mary Latimer Gambrell, *Ministerial Training in Eighteenth-Century New England* (New York: AMS, 1967), 83.

5. J. J. Van Oosterzee, *Practical Theology: A Manual for Theological Students* (London: Hodder and Stoughton, 1878), 62.

heralds of the Word of Life. As such it displays—however closely allied to the domain of art—the unequivocal character of a science, and one for the future minister of the Gospel absolutely indispensable. As such it is opposed only by ignorance and prejudice, although powerless in itself alone to form living and life-awakening witnesses of the Salvation in Christ.[6]

Andover Theological Seminary established the Bartlet Professorship of Sacred Rhetoric in 1808, provided by William Bartlet of Newburyport, Massachusetts.[7] The catalogs of Andover Theological Seminary from 1819 to 1830 demonstrate the key role of homiletics in the curriculum, with students' final year focusing on sermon development and the practice of preaching. Later, the 1850 catalog includes "Homiletics" and "Sermonizing."[8]

Princeton Theological Seminary, founded in 1812, appointed Samuel Miller in 1813 as the Professor of Ecclesiastical History and Church Government—"church government" meaning practical theology, including preaching. Miller lectured to third-year students on the practice of preaching.[9] The Princeton faculty considered pulpit eloquence so important that as early as 1858 the teaching of speech was added to the curriculum to supplement the teaching of preaching.[10]

Harvard established its Divinity School in 1815, and by 1830 announced the funding of the Professor of Pastoral Care and Pulpit Oratory, teaching students the composition and delivery of sermons. Students at the school

---

6. Oosterzee, *Practical Theology*, 62.

7. *General Catalogue of the Theological Seminary, Andover, Massachusetts, 1808–1908*, 15.

8. Robert L. Kelly, *Theological Education in America: A Study of One Hundred Sixty-One Theological Schools in the United States and Canada* (New York: Doran, 1924), 65–66.

9. James H. Moorhead, *Princeton Seminary in American Religion and Culture* (Grand Rapids: Eerdmans, 2012), 64, 73; William K. Selden, *Princeton Theological Seminary: A Narrative History 1812-1992* (Princeton, NJ: Princeton University Press, 1992), 18.

10. Charles L. Bartow, "In Service to the Servants of the Word: Teaching Speech at Princeton Seminary," *Princeton Seminary Bulletin* 13:3 (November 1992): 274. Bartow notes: "The earliest mention of teaching speech at Princeton Theological Seminary is in the catalogue of 1858–59. 'Special instruction and exercise in the art of Elocution, by the best qualified teachers in the country, at a very small expense to the student.' In the Princeton Seminary catalogue of 1866 mention is made of exercises in reading and sermon delivery without notes as part of the preaching requirement (p. 18). The catalogue also indicates that 'exercise in the art of Elocution, without charge to students' is available." See Bartow, 274.

were exposed to the value of preaching in the curriculum for the churches they would serve. The catalog states:

> A religious service, with preaching, in which one of the students officiates, takes place twice a week, and is attended by the Professors and all the members of the school. Also once a week there is an exercise in extemporaneous preaching, in the presence of one of the Professors, by the students of the two upper classes in rotation. Students take their turns in performing these exercises with the first term of the middle year.[11]

Another example of the prominent role of homiletics in the theological curriculum is Yale Divinity School, founded in 1822. By 1817 an informal divinity school was already functioning at the college with a few graduates who remained to study divinity. Yale's commitment to preaching is indicated as early as the appointment in 1817 of Chauncey Allen Goodrich as professor of rhetoric and oratory.[12] Then, by 1822 fifteen students of that year's graduating class requested to study divinity following graduation. Professor of divinity Eleazar T. Fitch supported their request to the administration to be formed into a regular theological class, thus providing the impetus for the founding of the divinity school.[13] The chair of homiletics was filled from 1822 to 1852 by Fitch, the Livingston Professor of Divinity.[14]

Other established seminaries later followed suit.[15] The Southern Baptist Theological Seminary was founded in 1859 in Greenville, South Carolina, and moved to Kentucky following the Civil War.[16] From its founding, John A. Broadus taught New Testament interpretation and homiletics. He is the author of *On the Preparation and Delivery of Sermons* (1870), one of the most influential trans-denominational textbooks on preaching in the

---

11. Kelly, *Theological Education in America*, 65.

12. Brooks Mather Kelly, *Yale: A History* (New London, CT: Yale University Press, 1974), 143–45.

13. Kelly, *Yale: A History*, 145–46.

14. Roland H. Bainton, *Yale and the Ministry* (San Francisco: Harper & Row, 1957), 83.

15. Richard J. Storr, *The Beginnings of Graduate Education in America* (New York: Arno, 1953).

16. Gregory A. Wills, *Southern Baptist Theological Seminary, 1859-2009* (New York: Oxford, 2009).

nineteenth and twentieth centuries.[17] In addition to The Southern Baptist Theological Seminary, Garrett Theological Seminary (1853), Rochester Theological Seminary (1850), Crozer Theological Seminary (1866), Union Theological Seminary [New York] (1836), Union Theological Seminary [Virginia] (1812), the Theological Seminary of the Reformed Church [New Brunswick Theological Seminary] (1784), Lutheran Theological Seminary in Philadelphia (1864), and Drew Theological Seminary (1867), among others, and more recently, Gordon Divinity School (1889), Trinity Evangelical Divinity School (1897), Southwestern Baptist Theological Seminary (1908), New Orleans Baptist Theological Seminary (1917), Dallas Theological Seminary (1924), Denver Seminary (1951), Beeson Divinity School (1988), and George W. Truett Theological Seminary (1993) required courses in homiletics for students as they prepared for ministry.[18]

In his expansive study of theological education in America, Robert Kelly observed the following concerning the teaching of preaching in various theological schools:

> Between these extremes of treatment, from the elementary one of method to the more profound one of thought and emotional expression, there are all kinds and quantities of work depending in some measure on facilities and size of staff. Among courses expressing current theory are the following: "modern preachers," illustrated with examples and studies of preachers of the present day; "biography"; "doctrinal preaching" (Union College) "made necessary by the modern tendency to slight fundamentals in favor of matter of a more popular character"; "doctrinal and expository preaching"

---

17. John A. Broadus, *On the Preparation and Delivery of Sermons*, ed. Edward Charles Dargan (New York: Harper & Brothers, 1870, 1898, 1926), i. See also *John A. Broadus: A Living Legacy*, ed. David S. Dockery and Roger D. Duke (Nashville: B&H, 2008), 68–96. Dargan, editor of the revised edition, notes: "The first edition of this work was published in the summer of 1870. … The book was a great success. It became the most popular and widely-read text-book on Homiletics in the country, and has passed through twenty-two editions [and] thousands of copies have been sold. It has been adopted in many theological seminaries of different denominations as the text-book, and in many where no text-book is used it is highly commended for study and reference. Besides this, it has had a wide and useful circulation among the ministry in general." Broadus, *On the Preparation and Delivery of Sermons*, ed. Dargan, i.

18. Kelly, *Theological Education*, 69, 78, 79, 81, 83, 136, 137. See also John D. Hannah, *An Uncommon Union: Dallas Theological Seminary and American Evangelicalism* (Grand Rapids: Zondervan, 2009), 78–79.

(Westminster Hall, Vancouver, BC); "preaching without manuscript"; "psychology of public presentation and adaptation to audiences, architecture and occasions" (Kimball School of Theology); "psychology of preaching" (Alfred Theological Seminary); "the preacher as a student" (Drake University College of the Bible); "sources of sermon material" (Evangelical Theological Seminary, Naperville, Illinois); "public prayer and public reading of the scriptures" (Western Theological Seminary, Pittsburgh); "addresses of Jesus, Peter, and Paul," "social teachings of Amos," "conversations of Jesus" (Newton Theological Institution). Union Theological Seminary begins brief sermons for second-year students only and goes on to six courses in doctrinal preaching and six in expository preaching. The Biblical Seminary in New York teaches homiletics in Italian for Italian students. Concordia Theological Seminary, Illinois, requires the preparation of some of the sermons in German. Suomi Synod requires that part of the work be in Finnish.[19]

Like the theological seminaries, Bible colleges and Bible institutes in the United States placed notable emphasis on the instruction and practice of preaching.[20] This brief survey indicates that from the beginning of theological education in the United States, homiletics served as one of the key components taught in the curriculum to strengthen a minister's education.

PROFESSORIAL DESIGNATIONS

The professor of preaching had various titles depending on the institution and the changing times. Since Christian homiletics was birthed in Greco-Roman rhetoric by Augustine the rhetorician,[21] rhetoric being one of the key components of learning (i.e., logic, rhetoric, and grammar), some institutions early on called their professor of preaching the "Professor of Sacred Rhetoric." For example, Andover Theological Seminary

---

19. Kelly, *Theological Education*, 137–38.

20. Neil Ayers Winegarden, "A Historical Survey of Homiletical Education in the United States" (ThD diss., Northern Baptist Theological Seminary, 1951).

21. *The Works of Aurelius Augustine, Bishop of Hippo*, ed. Marcus Dods, vol. 9, *On Christian Doctrine; The Enchiridion; On Catechesing; and On Faith and the Creed* (Edinburgh: T&T Clark, 1873); Richard Leo Enos and Roger Thompson, et al., eds., *The Rhetoric of St. Augustine of Hippo: De Doctrina Christiana and the Search for a Distinctly Christian Rhetoric* (Waco, TX: Baylor, 2008).

established the Bartlet Professorship of Sacred Rhetoric in 1808. The designation was changed in 1896 to Professor of Homiletics.[22] Similarly, Newton Theological Institution inaugurated the Professor of Sacred Rhetoric and Pastoral Duties, and in 1882 changed the title to Professor of Homiletics, Pastoral Duties and Church Polity. Nearly fifty years later, in 1929, the title then became Professor of Preaching.[23] Presently, titles for professors include Professor of Preaching,[24] Professor of Homiletics,[25] Professor of Preaching and Rhetoric,[26] Professor of Expository Preaching,[27] Professor of Communication,[28] Professor of Pastoral Studies,[29] and Professor of Christian Preaching.[30]

THE TRAINING OF PREACHERS FROM PAST TO PRESENT

As for the training of ministers in the task of preaching, there appear to be at least two approaches: apprenticeship and formal college-to-seminary instruction.

APPRENTICESHIP

From the early church onward, apprenticeship of ministers formed the practice of developing leadership for the local church. The discipleship of Timothy by the apostle Paul demonstrates a semiformal structure of

---

22. *General Catalogue of the Theological Seminary, Andover, Massachusetts, 1808–1908*, 15–16.

23. Richard Donald Pierce, ed., *General Catalogue of the Newton Theological Institution, 1826–1943: With Biographical Sketches of Professors and Students in Andover Theological Seminary, 1931–1943* (Newton Center, MA: The Newton Theological Institution, 1943), 24–29, 111, 116, 168.

24. For example, Gordon-Conwell Theological Seminary uses this title, http://www.gordonconwell.edu/academics/Faculty.cfm.

25. For example, Trinity Evangelical Divinity School, https://divinity.tiu.edu/academics/faculty-info/.

26. For example, some Southwestern Baptist Theological Seminary faculty members use this designation, https://swbts.edu/academics/faculty/preaching/.

27. For example, some New Orleans Baptist Theological Seminary faculty members use this designation, http://www.nobts.edu/faculty/itor/millerm.html.

28. For example, see Gordon-Conwell Theological Seminary and Southwestern Baptist Theological Seminary.

29. For example, Moody Bible Institute employs this designation, https://www.moody.edu/academics/faculty/.

30. For example, Beeson Divinity School uses this designation, https://www.beesondivinity.com/faculty.

pastoral training. Paul specifically instructs Timothy to train others as Paul has trained him: "And the things you have heard me say in the presence of many witnesses entrust to reliable people who will also be qualified to teach others" (2 Tim 2:2). This manner of instruction reflects Jesus' mandate to make disciples, "teaching them to obey everything I have commanded you" (Matt 28:20).

Augustine urged that preachers learn from other preachers, coming under the tutelage of an experienced preacher to learn how to preach. Augustine states, "For men of quick intellect and glowing temperament find it easier to become eloquent by reading and listening to eloquent speakers than by following rules for eloquence."[31] They are to do this "by learning words and phrases from those who do speak," by imitating models of eloquence.[32]

John Edwards, a British Puritan of the eighteenth century, noted that the preacher must be a:

> Linguist, a Grammarian, a Critick, an Orator, a Philosopher, and Historian, a Casuist, a Disputant, and whatever Speaks Skill and Knowledge in any Learned Science. ... He is to speak all Subjects, and therefore must be made up of all Knowledge and learning. For all Arts serve one another, so they serve Divinity too, and are someways requisite in a Preacher.[33]

The apprenticeship model was the custom of ministerial training during the colonial period. American clerical education included reading Samuel Willard's *Brief Directions to a Young Scholar Designing the Ministry for the Study of Divinity*, published posthumously in Boston in 1735. Willard was vice president of Harvard College from 1701–1707. Some private instruction by experienced pastors was given to students who completed the college course.

Jonathan Edwards likewise engaged in preparing ministers for the pulpit. Edwards considered preaching skills to be of some value but

---

31. Augustine, *On Christian Doctrine*, 122.

32. Augustine, *On Christian Doctrine*, 123. I'm grateful for Jared Alcántara's insight on this point.

33. John Edwards, *The Preacher*, 3 vols. (London: J. Robinson, J. Lawrence, and J. Wyat, 1705–1709), 1:268–69. Quoted in Gambrell, *Ministerial Training*, 17.

emphasized the mastery of doctrine.[34] Pastors William Tennent, Joseph Bellamy, Ezra Stiles, Nathanael Emmons, Ebenezer Porter, and John Smalley, among others, reflected this apprenticeship approach to training preachers in the late eighteenth and early nineteenth centuries.[35] Mary Gambrell's study of ministerial training in eighteenth-century New England indicates how mentees were taught to preach. For example, Nathanael Emmons's instruction on homiletics included the following:

> Emmons gave special advice on sermon construction, public speaking, parochial duties, and private conversation, making general recommendations as to subsequent independent preaching. Apparently he was particularly interested in, and gave special attention to, matters of style and delivery, vitally influencing methods of sermon construction in New England for half a century, notwithstanding the fact that he, himself, as previously noted, made an unattractive pulpit appearance.[36]

In addition to instruction by the mentor, students practiced and developed their preaching while supplying pulpits in the surrounding communities. Joseph Bellamy was one pastor who took novice preachers under his wing. One of Bellamy's students, Levi Hart, learned a valuable lesson from supply preaching with his teacher sitting in the congregation:

> He had made earnest preparation for his first pulpit appearance, and at its conclusion felt well pleased with is performance. As they rode home after the service, he and Bellamy side by side in front, followed by the other students in procession, Bellamy's silence on the subject of the sermon added to Hart's self-satisfaction. They discussed various topics, while those in the rear rode as closely as possible in order to catch the venerable teacher's remarks. At last, when near home, they passed a field of luxuriant buckwheat plants on which there was no grain. "Hart," the doctor called in stentorian tones, "You see that buckwheat? There is your sermon."[37]

---

34. Gambrell, *Ministerial Training*, 43–44.
35. Gambrell, *Ministerial Training*, 126.
36. Gambrell, *Ministerial Training*, 132–33.
37. Gambrell, *Ministerial Training*, 135.

Another contribution to the training of pastors was made by Cotton Mather. His *Manductio ad Ministerium*, published in 1726, served as a guide to college students. The work was republished in 1781 and 1789, and titled *Dr. Cotton Mather's Student and Preacher*.[38]

The apprenticeship model remained a way in which preachers were trained well after the founding of theological seminaries. Some who sensed the call to pastoral ministry avoided formal education, could not afford it, were educationally impaired or unprepared, or were hindered by age or any number of reasons. Many of these chose to be apprenticed to a seasoned pastor to train for ministry. Late nineteenth-century preacher Russell H. Conwell, the celebrated pastor of Grace Baptist Church in Philadelphia—also known as the Baptist Temple—did not choose the standard way to pastoral ministry. Instead, he was apprenticed by pastors and seminary professors.[39]

Apprenticeship in preaching is part of the legacy of African American preaching. Jared Alcántara helpfully notes:

> Throughout church history, scores of preachers have learned to preach through an apprenticeship model, the most obvious and pertinent example being the apprenticeship tradition in the black church. In other words, apprenticeship is not a new idea. It is an idea as old as preaching itself.[40]

Alcántara emphasizes, "A significant number of African American preachers today have learned to preach in an apprenticeship tradition."[41]

Apprenticeship in preaching is also reflected in other ethnic and denominational traditions. From Romanian Baptists to Hispanic Pentecostals, in traditions where formal training is either frowned upon or unattainable, apprenticeship in preaching is a long-practiced approach.[42] Rural pastors

38. Gambrell, *Ministerial Training*, 24.

39. See John R. Wimmer, "Symbols of Success: Russell H. Conwell and the Transformation of American Protestantism" (PhD diss., University of Chicago, 1992); Agnes Rush Burr, *Russell H. Conwell and His Work: One Man's Interpretation of Life* (Philadelphia: John C. Winston, 1917).

40. Jared E. Alcántara, *Learning from a Legend: What Gardner C. Taylor Can Teach Us about Preaching* (Eugene, OR: Cascade, 2016), 70.

41. Alcántara, *Learning*, 73.

42. Cultural and ethnic sensitivity to the availability of education and thoughtfulness to the ethnocentrism bound to approaches to teaching preaching are needed here. See Gerald

and urban preachers also continue the tradition of the apprenticeship model.[43] Collaborative homiletic instruction is another form of apprenticeship conducted in "communities of practice," where there are "supportive networks of reflective preaching practitioners, enhancing the provision of mentor-mentee relationships."[44]

SEMINARY INSTRUCTION

With the establishment of Harvard College in 1636 and the founding of Andover Theological Seminary in 1808, increased attention was given to an educated clergy. Undergraduates at Harvard studied Hebrew, as the curriculum intended to cultivate both mind and heart. They sat under godly preaching and engaged in devotions. Harry Stout explains:

> On Sundays students attended local churches, particularly the church at Cambridge, where they heard the best preaching in the land, which they later recited for practice. Surviving student notebooks contain complete collections of sermon notes that no doubt were invaluable when the young ministers came to fashion their own sermons. To complete biblical and homiletical training, the president of the college and master's students delivered biweekly declamations that defended "commonplaces" drawn from "divinity" rather than the classical loci communes. These speaking performances taught students how to combine logic and Scripture for the purpose of "avoiding and refuting" heretical teachings that might crop up in their reading or in the course of their parish ministries.[45]

T. du Preez, "Teaching Homiletics in a Multi-Cultural Context: A South African Perspective," 27th International Faith and Learning Seminar held at Mission College, Muak Lek, Thailand, December 3–15, 2000.

43. "Preachers' College," a two-and-a-half-day training for lay preachers conducted by the Haddon W. Robinson Center for Preaching at Gordon-Conwell Theological Seminary (South Hamilton, MA) demonstrates anecdotally this breadth of representation for the apprenticeship model. Preachers' College has been conducted for more than fifteen years with rural whites, urban blacks and Hispanics, immigrants from various nations, Baptists, Presbyterians, and Pentecostals attending. All participants are involved in lay, bivocational, or full-time pastoral-preaching ministry.

44. Geoffrey Stevenson, "Learning to Preach: Social Learning Theory and the Development of Christian Preachers" (PhD diss., University of Edinburgh, 2009), vii.

45. Stout, *The New England Soul*, 90.

Since the founding of Andover, students have first completed the undergraduate degree and then spent three years in the study of divinity. This has become the traditional approach to the training of ministers.[46]

Seminary students study biblical, theological, historical, and practical subjects. Preaching, as noted above, has been a long-time vital component of the curriculum. John McClure reflects on the place of preaching in the Presbyterian tradition:

> At the turn of the century, the typical homiletics curriculum in Presbyterian seminaries was an extensive, three-year process that involved the learning of "Sacred Rhetoric" or "theory of preaching," the studying and outlining of the English Bible, the learning of principles of elocution, and the practice of public speaking. For instance, in 1900 at Union Seminary in Richmond, Virginia, a student could expect to begin immediately in the junior year reading *On the Preparation and Delivery of Sermons* by Southern Baptist homiletician John Broadus. At the same time, students would learn homiletical theory in class. Then, during the second semester, the English Bible was studied and exercises in outlining would be practiced. At the same time the student would be required to take a course in "Training the Speaking Voice." For the next two years, each student would be required to take a semester of English Bible, studying and outlining the Old Testament during the middler year and the New Testament during the senior year. Students were also required to take a course in the "Oral Interpretation of the Bible" during their middler years and a course in "Sermon Delivery" during their senior year. At each stage of the process, opportunities to preach were provided to every student either in nearby churches or in the seminary chapel, often with several faculty members present to critique. Similar patterns and emphases could be found in other Presbyterian seminaries during this period, and only small revisions in curriculum were made until the mid-1930s.[47]

---

46. Glenn T. Miller, *Piety and Profession: American Protestant Theological Education, 1870–1970* (Grand Rapids: Eerdmans, 2007), 325.

47. John McClure, "Changes in the Authority, Method, and Message of Presbyterian (PCUSA) Preaching in the Twentieth Century," in *The Confessional Mosaic: Presbyterians and*

What McClure outlined above reflects some past and current practices in seminaries in the United States. In the seminary instruction approach, those preparing for ministry are provided a broad exposure to divinity and the opportunity to cultivate one's preaching as a key component of theological education.

The seminary instruction approach has remained the primary pathway for ministerial training in the last one hundred fifty years and as demonstrated in the current climate of theological education. However, with changes in attitudes toward theological education, online course growth, declining residential seminary trends, the rising cost of residential theological education, cultural shifts, and ministry training offered by the megachurch or other organizations, the future of seminary instruction appears to weigh in the balance.[48]

THE TRAINING AND SELECTION
OF HOMILETICS PROFESSORS

Making the case for the place of preaching and the preaching professor, Merrimon Cuninggim of Perkins School of Theology argued in 1955, "For homiletics is more than 'hints of the proper craft, tricks of the tool's true play'; it is, like every other area of theological study, the communication of the Christian Gospel."[49]

If Cuninggim is correct, and I think he is, a review of the ways in which preaching professors have come to the post of teaching homiletics will help in understanding today's context.

Twentieth-Century Theology, ed. Milton J. Coalter, John Mulder, and Louis B. Weeks (Louisville: Westminster John Knox, 1990), 93.

48. Concerns about the changes in theological education abound. See, for example, Jeremiah McCarthy, "Deepening Connections between the Church and the Theological School: Implications for Theological Education," *Journal of Adult Theological Education* 1:2 (2004): 175–83, http://www.tandfonline.com/doi/abs/10.1558/jate.1.2.175.65572; Barbara G. Wheeler and Anthony T. Ruger, "Sobering Figures Point to Overall Enrollment Decline: New Research from the Auburn Center for the Study of Theological Education," *In Trust* (Spring 2013): 5–11, http://www.intrust.org/Portals/39/docs/IT413wheeler.pdf.

49. Merrimon Cuninggim, "Changing Emphases in the Seminary Curriculum," *The Journal of Bible and Religion* 23:2 (April 1955): 117.

THE EXPERIENCED PASTOR PROFESSOR

A survey of the names of the professors who taught preaching in some of the first seminaries indicates they mainly came from the pastorate.[50] "It is perhaps natural that for teachers of pastoral theology men should be chosen who have been pastors," writes William Adams Brown in his exhaustive study of ministerial education in America.[51] Thomas Long notes:

> At one time, when a theological school needed a professor of church administration, preaching or worship, it searched the ranks of accomplished clergy. Often these seasoned practitioners did a capable job teaching the lore and wisdom of their craft. But they were sometimes less successful in conducting research, introducing innovations into their fields and participating in ongoing scholarly conversation.[52]

Drawing from the pastorate to fill a homiletics teaching position brings a wealth of pastoral ministry experience to the classroom. However, the candidate may not necessarily have expertise—or even an advanced degree—in the field of homiletics. They may be a fine preacher and teacher, but unable to show what makes a person effective in the preparation and delivery of sermons, thus lacking perspective and depth in the discipline.

The practice of drawing exclusively from the pastorate to fill preaching professor slots may have served well in the past, but may be less desirable in today's climate.

THE HOMILETICS GRADUATE STUDIES PROFESSOR

Haddon Robinson affirms that one of the most difficult positions to fill on a theological faculty is the preaching professor.[53] He notes that there are two reasons for this challenge. First, the preaching professor likes to preach

---

50. For example, Henry Jones Ripley was an evangelist and later pastor who taught preaching at Newton Theological Institution (1826–1857). See *A Tribute to the Memory of Rev. Henry J. Ripley D.D.* (Boston: Franklin Press, 1875). Arthur Savage Train was Professor of Sacred Rhetoric at Newton Theological Institution (1858–1860). He spent twenty-three years as pastor of First Baptist Church, Haverhill, Massachusetts, before teaching at Newton. See "Arthur Savage Train," The Forty-Third Anniversary of the Conference of Baptist Ministers, held with the Baptist Church in Clinton, October 29, 1872 (Boston: C. H. Simonds, 1897), 64–66.

51. William Adams Brown, *The Education of American Ministers*, vol. 1 of *Ministerial Education in America* (New York: Institute of Social & Religious Research, 1934), 109.

52. Thomas G. Long, "Teaching Vacancies," *The Christian Century* 24 (February 2004): 30.

53. Personal conversation with the author.

and is therefore drawn to the local church to preach regularly. Second, the local church tends to provide a more robust salary and benefits package than the seminary or Bible college.

In his fictional scenario about a seminary searching for a preaching professor, Thomas Long writes that the search committee's position description required a person to have a PhD and some pastoral ministry experience. They advertised the position and awaited responses. Whereas the New Testament search the year before yielded over sixty proven applicants, the homiletics search barely received a dozen applicants, and not a single one met the minimal requirements. Long observes, "Three years later, the committee is still looking."[54]

The Auburn Center for the Study of Theological Education observes two difficult forces that developed over the last twenty years in the practical theology fields. First, some professors in these fields left their posts because they retired, moved to churches where salaries were bigger, or changed organizations. In 2004 Long predicted, "This problem will become worse: an earlier Auburn study indicated that nearly 60 percent of the faculty now teaching in practical fields will be eligible to retire by 2006."[55]

The Auburn study stated that the second force was the higher standards for those teaching in practical fields set by the theological schools. Long comments, "Today teaching the arts of ministry requires a different kind of expertise, a different level of expertise, a different level of academic training and set of credentials."[56]

The strength of an academically trained professor of preaching can also be the weakness of an academically trained preaching professor who may know the field of homiletics but does not know people. Full-time experience as a pastor in a church would serve as the best remedy. Academic preparation is essential in today's economy. But equally important is the practical preparation of preaching week after week, putting into practice what one knows academically.

---

54. Long, "Teaching Vacancies," 30.
55. Long, "Teaching Vacancies," 30.
56. Long, "Teaching Vacancies," 30.

How should homiletics professors be selected and trained? I often tell colleagues that if I were in charge, I would require every professor who teaches at the seminary to have full-time pastoral ministry experience before coming on board to teach. Seminary students trained by professors with full-time pastoral ministry experience receive well-rounded teaching for serving as pastors. Without this experience, we in the academy tend to create disconnected silos of expertise rather than preachers who connect to people in the church and understand their needs. The end goal is not teaching in the classroom; it is beyond the classroom. The goal is the spiritual maturity of the church, the congregations students will pastor after they leave the school's hallowed halls. The ideal preaching professor is someone who has a firm experiential grasp of pastoral ministry—where preaching hits the highway—and a solid sense of the field of homiletics. This person has been both a pastor and a professor. They are not armchair quarterbacks. They have been there, and know from experience and from education what it means to preach.

Students considering a calling to teach homiletics often ask me what the best path to the classroom might be. Whether they go to graduate school or to the pastorate first is not the issue. Either way, they must keep in view that both elements will make a person the best suited teacher of preaching. Having these two components—pastoral ministry experience and advanced education—are incredible strengths. The only weakness I can perceive is becoming off balance in one's approach to teaching homiletics. Focusing on only one—the pastorate or the academy—will hinder effectiveness with students and, ultimately, the church.

CHALLENGES

There are challenges in promoting a robust recognition of the place of homiletics in the theological faculty and curriculum. Below I will discuss four: silos of expertise, faculty positions, faculty competence, and faculty professional challenges.

SILOS OF EXPERTISE

A longstanding issue in theological faculties is that the various disciplines tend to teach apart from each other. Merrimon Cuninggim complained in the middle of the twentieth century, "We of the seminaries' faculties do our work in relative isolation from each other."[57] Cuninggim continues, "The great majority of us have come to our seminary posts as ministers undertaking a specialized ministry in seminary teaching, rather than as educators undertaking a specialized teaching in theological education."[58] The matter of silos continues to the present. Some professors come to their posts as experts in the particular area of specialty but lack any meaningful pastoral experience that would prompt them to make the connections between the academy and the person sitting in the congregation.

FACULTY POSITIONS

It appears that in some theological schools and Bible colleges, preaching is not considered to be on the same level as other theological disciplines as the homiletics teaching slot is typically filled with an adjunct professor who may be a fine practitioner but may not know the field. An informal website search for those holding preaching faculty positions in seminaries and Bible colleges suggests the preponderance of adjuncts as the main teachers of homiletics at a number of institutions.[59] Additionally, turnover in preaching positions seems to loom large. A commitment by academic administration to the place of the discipline of preaching and the hiring of full-time professors may begin to turn these trends around coupled with the retention of qualified faculty and adjuncts, which is key.

FACULTY COMPETENCE, OR "ANYONE CAN TEACH PREACHING"

Some schools have appointed homiletics professors because they demonstrate skill as an effective preacher, not because of their competence in the field of preaching. H. Grady Davis observed this practice of faculty appointment to teach preaching as an issue in 1960. He notes that this person "is now teaching homiletics because the curriculum calls for homiletics and

---

57. Cuninggim, "Changing Emphases," 111–12.

58. Cuninggim, "Changing Emphases," 110–11.

59. A casual web search on preaching faculties in various institutions will demonstrate this to be the case. See, for example, Evangelical Theological Seminary, Myerstown, Pennsylvania, https://evangelical.edu/about/faculty/.

the school has no professor better qualified to teach it."[60] Work must be done to cultivate the need for homileticians in the field and to develop academic pathways for those who sense a call to teach preaching in seminaries, Bible colleges, or mission organizations.

FACULTY PROFESSIONAL CHALLENGES

Professors of preaching may not be involved academically and practically with other professors of preaching. The Evangelical Homiletics Society, founded in 1997, is an essential professional organization with which to connect. The society publishes a peer-reviewed journal twice a year. To develop the field of homiletics, teachers of preaching need to be involved in their guild and strive to connect regularly with others who are actively working in their field.[61]

WHERE DO WE GO FROM HERE?
DEVELOPING THE FIELD OF HOMILETICS

Historically, the field of homiletics as an academic discipline has faced challenges, ignorance, and opposition. In his monumental 1934 study of the education and training of American ministers, William Adams Brown outlined his concerns for the development of teaching preaching and the field of homiletics:

> There are, in particular, three needs for which provision must be made in any comprehensive and well-balanced program. There is (1) the need of adequate provision for the education of the specialist, both in the field of administration and of teaching. There is (2) the need of providing facilities for continued education of those persons—whether ministers or laymen—whose past training in religion has been defective. There is (3) the need of first-hand research in fields where the contemporary church faces problems of major importance and difficulty.[62]

---

60. Henry Grady Davis, "The Teaching of Homiletics: The Present Situation in American Seminaries," *Encounter* 22 (Spring 1961): 205.

61. For more information, see https://ehomiletics.com.

62. William Adams Brown, *The Education of American Ministers*, vol. 1 of *Ministerial Education in America* (New York: Institute of Social and Religious Research, 1934), 209.

In his study of the teaching of homiletics in American seminaries in 1960, H. Grady Davis observed similar voices of discontent among those who taught preaching that may also be heard in the current climate. Among the preaching professors involved in the study, Davis noted, "There was apparently a majority opinion that improvement depends on developing homiletics as an integrated field for graduate studies, including all the essential contributory disciplines, and leading to a doctorate."[63] Davis further stated, "The need is that schools and teachers of homiletics take seriously the problem with which the present situation confronts them."[64]

In the same way, Thomas Long issues this call concerning the development of teachers of preaching and other practical fields:

> In a climate of global awareness, practical theology is not only deeper but also broader. There is an increasing alertness to how the church's ministries of teaching, worship, preaching, education, and leadership connect to the practices of other world religions, to the practices of religious communities throughout history, and to parallel practices in the wider culture.[65]

CONCLUSION

This chapter has demonstrated the important place of teachers of preaching throughout the generations as well as the significant role the discipline of homiletics has had and will continue to have.

The future of homiletics teaching is rich, bright, and abundant with possibilities in the church, in the seminary or Bible college, or in missions—both local and global. The church needs to hear a clear word from God. As a crafter of the mouthpieces of the Lord in the students you serve, you have the privilege of shaping a generation to proclaim God's authoritative word.

And although there are challenges, you have a job to do: teach others to preach.

---

63. Davis, "The Teaching of Homiletics," 206.
64. Davis, "The Teaching of Homiletics," 206.
65. Long, "Teaching Vacancies," 30.

2

o o o

An Apology for Learning Educational Theory

PATRICIA M. BATTEN

Instructors need a bridge between research and
practice, between teaching and learning.[1]

55150. I can't tell you how many times I punched in that sequence of numbers on the Konica 520 keypad.

I came to the teaching profession ten years ago, in a roundabout sort of
way. I filled in for a professor who was going on sabbatical. Given several
months to prepare, my professor friend had time to show me the ropes. I
found myself with his notes and his PowerPoint slides and the department
code for the copy machine; 55150 will forever be etched in my mind. But
this professor didn't simply hand me a three-ring binder and walk away.
He cared deeply about how his preaching course was taught. It was the
basic course in preaching. The fundamentals. The ten stages of expository
preaching. If students didn't learn the basics in this course, they'd have
a difficult task not only in the next required preaching course, but also
in a parish pulpit ministry context. I realized the magnitude of my task
compared to my complete lack of teaching experience. I needed to teach
beginners how to preach the word of God. It was a serious job and I was
scared. My professor friend sat down with me many times, and together
we worked through a teaching plan. Scott M. Gibson is still investing in
me today. I'm forever grateful.

The next semester, I took on the role of assisting the professor who
wrote our preaching textbook. For five years, I attended every class Haddon

---

1. Susan Ambrose et al., *How Learning Works: Seven Research-Based Principles for Smart Teaching* (San Francisco: Jossey Bass, 2010), 2.

Robinson taught. I've been through his Practice and Principles of Preaching course eight times, not including the time I took it for credit as a student. Credit hours flew by and Haddon gave me more and more opportunities to teach. He wasn't shy about letting me know if my teaching worked or if it fell flat.

I was teaching preaching. And I learned from the best.

But something was still missing.

Given my own courses to teach, I was confused—even frustrated—by mixed student achievement. Some students faced course objectives with bravery, tackling their preaching fears head-on, while others lacked the courage to conquer the curriculum. I wasn't consistently connecting with my students. One class session felt like a success while another, a failure— and I didn't know why. Some students grasped what I taught while others never fully did. Still others slumped in their chairs, avoiding eye contact by hiding behind a laptop. I knew the problem wasn't related to content. I understood the material. I had a firm grasp of homiletics. The problem was that I had a one-size-fits-all approach to teaching it.

I discovered that I really didn't know a thing about my audience. I gave my students an information dump. I could fire-hose them with lessons on expository preaching, but I never asked *how* students learn, or better yet, how *particular students* learn, or how might I change my teaching to help the students sitting right in front of me.

WHO IS MY AUDIENCE?

The first question any preacher worth her salt asks when preparing to preach is, "Who is my audience?" It still amazes me that I taught an entire course geared toward preaching and the audience, Preaching to the Modern Listener, but I never thought of my students as an audience I needed to exegete. Then it occurred to me that preachers should be the best teachers. They simply need to do in the classroom what they do in the pulpit. They need to analyze their audience—their students.

Educational theory is interested in the audience, the student. There are two components to educational theory: how people learn (the science of learning) and how to help people learn (the science of instruction).

Preachers never enter the pulpit without a sense of knowing who sits in the pews before them. They ask all kinds of questions of their preaching audience to find out who they are. They analyze their cultural, ethnic, socioeconomic, and educational background. They're interested in their political stripes. They analyze where they stand spiritually. Are they fully devoted followers? Are they seekers? Are they somewhere in between? They try to analyze how they might respond to the message. Will they be suspicious? Apathetic? Enthusiastic?

They recognize that most American audiences are poor listeners and they know that attention is fleeting, so they take that into consideration before preaching. Preachers make certain homiletical decisions based on how they know audiences listen. They write introductions that gain attention and surface need. They use narrative to draw people in and capture their imaginations. They make use of repetition. They organize their thoughts inductively to elicit an emotional response or deductively when they want to be super clear.

Preachers know how to analyze an audience. But for some reason, when they walk into the classroom as teachers, their students are strangers. They may know generally who they are. But they haven't done the rigorous work of analyzing their student audience. More specifically, they haven't concerned themselves with how students learn. Their one-size-fits-all approach to teaching is one that they'd unequivocally reject in the pulpit.

WHY DO WE TEACH THE WAY WE TEACH?

Several years ago, I gave a take-home assignment to my students on Peter's Pentecost sermon in Acts 2. It was the same assignment my predecessor used. It was labor-intensive, analyzing the homiletics of Peter's message. I graded the assignments and then reviewed them with my students in class. It seemed clear that many students were more concerned with their grade than what they were learning in Acts 2. I thought it was an important assignment, so I decided to change my teaching approach.

Today, Peter's Pentecost sermon is still in the syllabus, but now my students analyze it as a group. I divide the class into small groups of three or four students, who take the assignment section by section. They wrestle with it first on a smaller scale before we bring it back to the larger group for discussion. Small groups now learn from other small groups. I facilitate the discussion, which sometimes gets rather heated!

This change in approach worked. Students now interact with one another and are engaged with the material. They seem to be learning. I am glad I changed the way students examine Acts 2, but it was really just a shot in the dark. I didn't understand why the change was positive. I didn't know about *synergogy*.

The idea behind synergogy is that learning that occurs in a group exceeds the learning that occurs as an individual. The aspect of competition is eliminated.

Learning has traditionally been understood as something that occurs within an individual, but even this concept has evolved over time. Think of your course on homiletics. You ask your class to break into groups of three or four students. You give them a biblical text, like Philippians 4:4–7. They need to determine the central idea of the passage. One student pulls out her iPad, another fires up his laptop. Bible software will even show them the occurrence of certain words, like "joy," throughout Philippians.

The individuals in the group are still learning, but learning is occurring within a community of practice that involves the knowledge and experience of other students as well as the aid of technology. A "community of learners" exists in which learning is distributed among individuals and enhanced with outside materials such as Bible software. The student is not learning entirely on his or her own, but is taking advantage of the knowledge and experience of other students and/or available technology (materials).

True, sometimes preaching teachers do things in class that just seem to work, and they're completely unaware of what larger theory lies behind the practice. But this method of lesson planning is haphazard. It's luck of the draw. Hit or miss. Knowing the theory behind the practice helps instructors target their teaching and increase student learning.

HOW DO WE BRIDGE THE GAP BETWEEN THEORY AND PRACTICE?

Research shows that some teaching methods are better than others, yet colleges and universities don't spend a lot of resources measuring teaching effectiveness.[2] Professors are left alone, wandering in the wilderness of educational theory. Accessing educational theory, come to find out, can be an overwhelming task. In discussing the difficulty in implementing effective teaching practices in higher education in the United States, Dean of Stanford's Graduate School of Education Dan Schwartz says: "The literature on how to do this stuff is a giant mountain of goo. I can tell people they need to teach better, but if I don't give them things that are easy for them to implement, they won't do it. And that's the same story in K–12 as it is in college."[3] Other scholars argue that the research of educational theory and the practice of teaching are disconnected. Angela Duckworth, author of *Grit: The Power and Passion of Perseverance*, says: "There's a yawning gap between a scientific study that shows that something is effective and a teacher knowing what to do Monday morning in the classroom."[4]

In a 4x6 wooden frame perched on Haddon Robinson's desk was a little ditty: "Tommy Snooks and Bessie Brooks were leaving church one Sunday. Said Tommy Snooks to Bessie Brooks, 'Tomorrow will be Monday'." That fine piece of poetry was dealing with application. What is preached on Sunday must make a difference on Monday. But for teachers of preaching, the ditty might be rewritten: "Tommy Snooks and Bessie Brooks were leaving school one Monday. Said Tommy Snooks to Bessie Brooks, 'Next week will be Sunday'." What professors of preaching do on Monday morning matters on Sunday morning. Robinson once told me he would impact preaching more by teaching students to preach, rather than by preaching in a regular parish pulpit ministry context.

What preaching teachers do on Monday morning makes a difference on Sunday morning. Teaching can make a difference in pulpits across America and around the globe. My hope is to motivate you to invest in learning educational theory—and the remaining chapters in this book will make that impossible mountain of goo look more like a hike-able hill.

---

2. Eric Westervelt, "Stanford Physicist Embarks on Mission to Improve Undergraduate Teaching," *NPR*, http://www.npr.org/2016/04/13/474120877/stanford-physicist-embarks-on-mission-to-improve-undergraduate-teaching.

3. Westervelt, "Stanford."

4. Angela Duckworth, "Grit and the Power of Perseverance," *OnPoint* (blog), May 2, 2016, http://www.wbur.org/onpoint/2016/05/02/angela-duckworth-on-grit-and-the-power-of-perseverance.

PINPOINT THE RESEARCH PRINCIPLE
TO TARGET YOUR TEACHING

When the science of learning and the science of instruction intersect, a classroom can be a vibrant place of learning. Students' motivation determines, directs, and sustains what they do to learn—a researched-based principle that has impacted my personal teaching of homiletics. According to Susan Ambrose et al., "When students find positive value in a learning goal or activity, expect to successfully achieve a desired learning outcome, and perceive support from their environment, they are likely to be strongly motivated to learn."[5]

Motivation refers to the personal investment a student makes in achieving goals. Maehr and Meyer elaborate, "Investment is seen in the direction, intensity, persistence, and quality of what is done and expressed."[6] Motivation researchers are interested in "the choices that people make among things to do, the persistence in those choices, the quality of behavior exhibited as they engage." Motivation, they argue, is the "sine qua non for learning. It is at the heart of what schools are about."[7] It is an enduring subject, the core of teaching and learning.[8]

Even without researching the topic of motivation, it was still easy to recognize that some students were more motivated than others. Research reveals three areas that contribute to student motivation: (1) Students must find value in preaching, (2) they must believe they can actually achieve the goal of preparing and delivering an expository sermon, and (3) they must feel that the learning environment is a supportive one.[9]

Imagine this scenario: it's the first day of a basic course in preaching and class begins with introductions. Everyone is given the opportunity to introduce themselves and talk about their goals for the course.

In my class, students share one hope they have for the class and one fear:

---

5. Ambrose et al., *How Learning Works*, 5.

6. M. Maehr and H. Meyer, "Understanding Motivation and Schooling: Where We've Been, Where We Are, and Where We Need to Go," *Educational Psychology Review* 9, no. 4 (1997): 373.

7. Maehr and Meyer, "Understanding Motivation," 377–78.

8. Maehr and Meyer, "Understanding Motivation," 372.

9. See Ambrose et al., *How Learning Works*. See also A. Wigfield and J. Eccles, "Expectancy-Value Theory of Achievement Motivation," *Contemporary Educational Psychology* 25 (2000): 68–81.

"My name is Andrew. I grew up in a strong Christian home. My dad's a pastor. I went to Bible college, where I took two preaching classes. Preaching is my passion. My hope is to build on what I already know about homiletics."

"My name is Kyle. I became a Christian in college. I've never preached a sermon in my life, but I want to be an effective communicator because I first trusted Jesus after I heard Andy Stanley preach at North Point. It changed my life."

"My name is Rebekah. I hope to pursue PhD studies after graduation. I don't expect to be in parish pulpit ministry, but this is a requirement. My goal is to pass with a grade that won't hurt my GPA."

"My name is Steve. I already have a job lined up working in Bible translation in Ghana. My missionary agency wanted me to take a preaching course, but I'm a 'behind-the-scenes' kind of guy. I love working in the original languages and I don't see myself ever preaching. I've got a heavy load of exegesis courses this semester."

"I'm Wes. I took a public speaking class in college and completely froze when I got up in front of the class. My hope is that I don't pass out while I preach."

"My name is Bruce. I've been pastor of Hope Christian Church for eight years. I've never taken an official preaching course, but I preach every Sunday! I work full time, and my wife and I are raising four kids—three boys and one girl. I hope to improve my preaching. My deacons sent me here."

"I'm Susan. I don't have any experience in preaching, but I want to learn. I'm definitely nervous."

Then I introduce myself:

"I'm Pat. I'm the course instructor. I place a high value on expository preaching. I think this is one of the most important classes you'll ever take in seminary. Preaching is crucial to an effective parish pulpit ministry. You'll gain a greater appreciation for God's word as you learn the stages of expository preaching."

I start the class this way because most students are anxious about taking this course. They're nervous about preaching in front of their peers. I want to show everyone that they're all in the same boat. I try to create a supportive environment because doing so is a key element toward student motivation.

UNDERSTANDING OUR AUDIENCE'S GOALS

Knowing theory helps preaching teachers to understand their students' goals. Many students come to the course simply wanting to pass the final or "get a good grade on the sermon." Their instructors, however, want them to learn how to effectively communicate God's word to people who are in desperate need of salvation and spiritual growth. Teachers and students have different goals. Just because the teacher states the course objective on the syllabus doesn't mean that the student is committed to that objective to the same degree as the instructor. Both may be seeking different levels of learning. As a professor, you have learning goals—your students might have performance goals.

Look at Rebekah's goals for the course. She may have "performance-approach goals" as opposed to "learning goals" when it comes to the course. Performance-approach goals "focus on attaining competence by meeting normative standards."[10] Rebekah's main concern is her GPA. She wants to learn the material for the test, not understand it for life. This means she may approach studying for the course in a different way than someone who has learning goals, like Andrew or Kyle. Students who are guided by learning goals "try to gain competence and truly learn what an activity or task can teach them."[11] These students will work hard to understand the material and apply it in a ministry context.

But there may be a student or two whose goal is not to work hard, but rather to "hardly work." These students have "work-avoidant goals." Like Steve, they want to finish work as quickly as possible with the least amount of effort. It's likely Steve doesn't approach all his courses with a work-avoidant mindset, but this course doesn't have great value to him. He's confident

---

10. Ambrose et al., *How Learning Works*, 71–72.

11. Ambrose, et al., *How Learning Works*, 72.

he won't be in a preaching ministry, so he'll spend more time and make a greater effort in his New Testament exegesis courses.

Instructors of preaching can help both Rebekah and Steve see the value in learning preaching. If they value expository preaching, then their goals might shift from a performance- or work-avoidant approach to a learning-goals approach.

In fact, research shows that the value assigned to a goal corresponds to motivation.[12] Motivation is the "personal investment that an individual has in reaching a desired state or outcome."[13] If a high value is placed on learning to preach effective expository sermons, then the student will be highly motivated to learn and understand the material in a lasting way, because "people are motivated to engage in behaviors to attain goals that have a high relative value."[14]

Knowing the relationship between the value of goals and motivation may encourage preaching teachers to rethink course lectures. Instead of diving directly into "Determining the Exegetical Idea," perhaps a class that deals with the "Value of Expository Preaching" might be a good starting point.

Let's go back to our student introductions. Steve, Kyle, and Susan are highly motivated students. They value their goals to learn expository preaching. They want to learn. They even expect to master the material.

Outcome expectancies are another contributing factor of motivation. When a student expects that they can successfully achieve course goals, motivation (personal investment student makes in reaching outcomes) increases. People are "motivated to pursue goals and outcomes that they believe they can successfully achieve."[15]

But Susan feels that the environment is not one in which she will thrive. The class is dominated by men. The professor seems stern. She fears how she will be critiqued during sermon feedback—by classmates and by the professor. She's not sure how the men in her class view women and preaching. She values the goal of learning to preach expository sermons. She is

12. See A. Wigfield and J. Eccles, "Expectancy-Value Theory of Achievement Motivation," *Contemporary Educational Psychology* 25 (2000): 68–81.

13. Ambrose et al., *How Learning Works*, 68.

14. Ambrose et al., *How Learning Works*, 74.

15. Ambrose et al., *How Learning Works*, 78. See also A. Bandura, *Self-Efficacy: The Exercise of Control* (New York: Freeman, 1977).

confident she can achieve the objective, but she finds the environment unsupportive.

Values and expectancies influence motivation, but so does the perception of one's environment. "Without question, the complex dynamics of the classroom, its tone, the interpersonal forces at play, and the nature and structure of communication patterns all combine to either support or inhibit the students' motivation to pursue a goal. If students perceive the environment as supportive (for example, "The instructor is approachable and several of my classmates seem willing to help me if I run into trouble"), motivation is likely to be enhanced. If students perceive the environment as unsupportive (for example, "This instructor seems hostile to women in engineering"), it can threaten expectations for success and erode motivation."[16]

Taking time for introductions during the first class meeting helps to create a supportive environment for learning. Students should be familiar with one another and familiar with the instructor. Professors of homiletics should make it clear from the start that they are approachable to all students and that they desire each and every student to be able preach effective expository sermons. They should be committed to teaching each student to become faithful expositors of God's word.

Additionally, other students may not feel they can meet course objectives. Wes may value the course and feel that the environment is supportive, but he's not sure he can meet the objectives based on his prior experience in a public speaking course, in which he fainted.

Because there will be students like Wes taking preaching courses every semester, it's important to prepare for those students by doing a couple of things. First, make sure the syllabus and course objectives are clear.[17] "When the instructional intent has been clarified—and revealed to the students—it is no longer necessary for them to guess what an instructor might have in mind for them to accomplish."[18] When course objectives are clear, students are more likely to believe that they can achieve course goals. If they don't understand what the professor requires, then they'll approach

---

16. Ambrose, et al., *How Learning Works*, 79.

17. See chapters 7 and 8 of this book.

18. Robert Mager, *Preparing Instructional Objectives* (Atlanta: Center for Effective Performance, 1997), 16.

the course with frustration and a sense that they will not be able to succeed in the course.

I start each semester by reviewing the syllabus. Even so, the color drains from students' faces when they see the phrase "preach without the use of notes." Immediately they think that they cannot meet that requirement. If a student starts my course by thinking he will fail, motivation to learn to preach will decrease. I must therefore increase student confidence in meeting the requirement to preach without notes.

The second thing professors can do to help students gain confidence is give them a smaller assignment that's due right away—one they are certain to achieve. Students need a win. They need a small victory early on in the course.

Familiarity with this research is why it is critical to take precious time at the beginning of the course to review the syllabus in depth and it's the reason to consider adding a shorter speaking assignment early on in the course. It's the reason for spending painstaking hours writing a new lecture on "The Value of Expository Preaching," and it's the reason why preaching teachers agonize over the wording of objectives. Knowing this research is the reason instructors must be approachable and it's the reason why they make every effort to create an environment that fosters respect and cares for each and every one of their students.

CONCLUSION

Educational theory deals with the science of learning and the science of instruction. Knowing what motivates students to learn—value, expectancy, and supportive environment—should make a difference in how instructors teach preaching.

A couple of user-friendly books will make your task achievable. You might pick up a copy of *How Learning Works* to dig into more research-based principles of learning, or you might order a copy of *Preparing Instructional Objectives* or *Understanding by Design*. In regard to creating a supportive environment for your learning theory, this book is a start. College-level professors and those who teach at the graduate level are not required to take courses in education. A support structure for learning theory doesn't exist for most professors in their particular teaching context. This book begins to create an environment of support for professors of preaching who value the idea that it's crucial to know how one's student audience learns.

I hope I've motivated you to learn more about how your student audience learns. Maybe, after reading this book, you'll come to value the role that educational theory can play in your teaching of homiletics because what you do on Monday morning matters on Sunday morning. Just ask Tommy Snooks and Bessie Brooks.

3

. . .

Help from Educational Theorists for Teaching Preaching

VICTOR ANDERSON

Do we teach homiletics or do we teach students?[1]

In the early 1990s, I saw myself simply as a practitioner of theological education. Striving to teach Bible, theology, and homiletics at a budding Bible college in Addis Ababa, Ethiopia, I spent little time pondering the esoteric musings of educational theorists. Frankly, I felt I would profit little by investing in abstract theories that did not help me navigate the challenges of teaching a full slate of courses in a cross-cultural context. I found great satisfaction in using traditional educational methods to help students learn content, pass exams, and develop new skills. My own expertise with the subject matter seemed to be increasing, so it was easy to assume that I was becoming a better educator. Amid these successes, however, I began to question if my approaches, embraced completely because of my own countless hours as a student, would have a positive long-term effect on my own students. The question became particularly vexing as I taught homiletics. I eventually reached the unsettling conclusion that I had little basis for evaluating what I was doing in the classroom. I needed help. Then came a question that provoked me to pursue assistance from educational theory.

"Do we teach the Bible, or do we teach students?" The question, posed as the title of an article written by educator James Plueddemann, hit me like a punch in the gut. While Plueddemann's article stimulated in me more questions than it answered, it catapulted me on a quest for educational theory

---

1. James E. Plueddemann, "Do We Teach the Bible, or Do We Teach Students?" *Christian Education Journal* 10, no. 1 (1989).

that provides a solid foundation for my current work as an educator.[2] In the twenty years since encountering that article, I have investigated how the practice of education can best proceed in the tension between content mastery and student orientation. This chapter, gleaning from those years of investigation and experimentation, focuses Plueddemann's concern specifically on the matter of teaching homiletics: Do we teach homiletics, or do we teach students?

Teachers of homiletics may have had little time or interest in delving into educational theories. At the same time, they intuitively recognize there is more to teaching homiletics than simply pushing content at students and pressing them into a particular preaching mold. You desire to teach *students*. But the sit-and-soak models that characterize most classroom experiences in higher education seem ill-fitted for the learning of homiletical theory and preaching skills. If such a description strikes a chord in your educational soul, this chapter is for you. I proceed from the foundational acknowledgment that teaching resides in the interplay between culturally approved content, individual learners, and ever-changing cultural contexts. The preaching teacher's theory and practice must simultaneously grasp the three poles.

In this chapter, the exploration of educational theory is organized around three questions related to education for adults, each question constructed to introduce a prominent theorist:

1. *What is learning?* This question initiates the discussion because one cannot consider the task of teaching without having a firm grip on what it means to learn and how that process may occur.

2. *How does dialogue influence the learning of homiletics?* Learning is fundamentally a dialogical process in which language plays a critical role. Yet in the traditional institutional setting, healthy dialogue may be a rarity. This question explores

---

2. Plueddemann's article was first presented as a paper titled "Is Teaching Theology an Art or a Science?" (1988) at a regional gathering of the Evangelical Theological Society at Taylor University. It was later published in *Christian Education Journal* 10, no. 1 (1989), and subsequently reprinted in *Africa Journal of Evangelical Theology* 13, no. 1 (1994).

both the value of and the prerequisites for using dialogue in education for homiletics.

3. *How does the culture of education affect the teaching and learning of homiletics?* This question explores the reality that education is situated in a cultural context with all its latent expectations and demands. Education is influenced by culture, has its own culture, and creates vision for changing culture.

The answers to each question provide a thumbnail sketch of theoretical concepts along with insights on possible applications to the teaching of homiletics. The chapter's limited scope means that details of each theory will be examined only to the extent needed to grapple with potential impacts on course design and execution. I encourage you to pursue original sources to increase your understanding of the theories. You'll gain an appreciation for how educational theory can help you teach homiletics more effectively and motivation to apply at least some of the theory directly into your course design and teaching methods.

WHAT IS LEARNING?

Teachers of homiletics inevitably find themselves at the intersection of theory and practice. While grappling with ideas of rhetoric (theory), theology, psychology, etc., they relentlessly seek connections to direct, applied experience (practice). In this world that constantly requires integration of ideas and experience, it makes sense that education is best conceived as connected to experience. This connection is not passive; rather, conceptualization and experience are always coupled through *experiential learning*. The work of David A. Kolb may well establish the clearest starting point for a foundational understanding of the theory.[3] I will briefly explore key tenets of Kolb's work to establish a framework for learning and then proceed with implications for teaching homiletics.

---

3. David A. Kolb, *Experiential Learning: Experience as the Source of Learning and Development* (Englewood Cliffs, NJ: Prentice-Hall, 1984). Kolb traces the roots of experiential learning theory from Dewey through Lewin, Piaget, and Bruner. He also notes significant contributions from therapeutic psychologies (Jung, Erikson, Rogers, Perls, and Maslow), radical educators (Freire and Illich), and brain research (Levy). Since Kolb's seminal work in 1984, numerous others have advanced experiential learning and its related disciplines.

Kolb provides the following succinct yet powerful definition of learning: "Learning is the process whereby knowledge is created through the transformation of experience."[4] Kolb's definition focuses on learning as a process. Learning, and thus helping others learn, is not fundamentally about a subject. It is a series of experiences that results in the creation of knowledge. The definition invites consideration of the nature of knowledge itself and the nature of learning experiences.

THE NATURE OF KNOWLEDGE

Knowledge is *created*. In the words of Jerome Bruner, it is *constructed*: "The 'reality' that we impute to the 'worlds' we inhabit is a constructed one. To paraphrase Nelson Goodman, 'Reality is made, not found'."[5] Creation of knowledge stands in stark contrast to the assumption that knowledge is acquired or received.[6] One does not obtain knowledge from the outside. Knowledge is not simply transferred from the professor (or author) into the mind of the student. Teaching, therefore, should not be likened to programming a computer or writing on blank slates or filling empty cups. Students are not banks into which professors make knowledge deposits.[7] All such metaphors of teaching fail because they proceed from a misunderstanding about the nature of knowledge. Knowledge is always created in the minds of individuals. And its existence in minds, rather than on paper or hard drives, brings with it both wonders and peculiarities.

Kolb's definition of learning provides a second insight into the nature of knowledge. It is idiosyncratic—that is, each person has his or her own knowledge. It is personal and in some respects unique. No two people have the exact same knowledge. This statement is not an admission to runaway relativism, nor does it suggest that all knowledge contributes equally valid renditions of reality. Rather, it is a realization that people have different

---

4. Kolb, *Experiential Learning*, 38.

5. Jerome Bruner, *The Culture of Education* (Cambridge, MA: Harvard University Press, 1996), 19–20.

6. For a helpful discussion of constructivism in its historical relation between epistemology and education, see Nel Noddings, *Philosophy of Education* (Boulder, CO: Westview Press, 1998).

7. Paulo Freire popularized the term "banking education," in which student responsibility revolves around receiving, filing, and storing the information deposited in them by their teachers. Paulo Freire, *Pedagogy of the Oppressed* (New York: Continuum, 1993).

minds and have encountered unique experiences from which they create their knowledge. Language and shared experience provide means for interaction and making meaning of shared knowledge. But shared meaning among individuals does not equate to uniform knowledge.

A third insight about the nature of knowledge may be gleaned from Kolb's definition. If knowledge is created by the transformation of experience, then learning is rooted in experience itself. No one can escape it. Learning and experience go hand in hand. That experience may come through direct apprehension or through less-direct comprehension, but a person's encounter with experience is at work as a determinative factor in the creation of knowledge. Further, adult learners come to any new learning experience with their own package of previous learning experiences resident in their memories (whether consciously or not). These previous learning experiences will interact with a new learning experience via assimilation or accommodation.[8] In less technical terms, educators must recognize that learners are constantly integrating new learning experiences with former ones, and affirming, building upon, and/or interpreting each set of experiences in relation to the others.

In sum, knowledge is created, idiosyncratic, and rooted in experience. As such, it should not be described in terms of outcomes. As Kolb states, it cannot be measured in terms of fixed ideas a person has accumulated. Learning is not, therefore, "obtaining knowledge of a storehouse of facts or habits representing behavioral responses to specific stimulus conditions."[9] What then, does it mean to go about learning? The next section explores the nature of learning itself.

THE NATURE OF LEARNING

Kolb's definition of learning influences understanding of the nature of learning itself. There are two elements of the learning process: the encounter

---

8. The terms "assimilation" and "accommodation" were used by Jean Piaget to describe how individuals respond to new learning experiences. In linking these ideas to experiential learning, Kolb provides the following insight. "In Piaget's terms, the key to learning lies in the mutual interaction of the process of accommodation of concepts or schemas to experience in the world and the process of assimilation of events and experiences from the world into existing concepts and schemas. Learning, or in Piaget's term, intelligent adaptation results from a balanced tension between these two processes" (Kolb, *Experiential Learning*, 23).

9. Kolb, *Experiential Learning*, 27.

with experience and the transformation of that experience. First, learning begins with an experiential encounter.[10] Kolb's framework splits these encounters into two types: apprehension or comprehension. The former is realized through direct concrete experience. This might be called an "in-your-face" experience, as when a swim instructor tells a novice swimmer, "Jump into the pool." The result is often an assault on the person's sensory system. In formal education, apprehension is generally reserved for laboratory or field experiences, outside the traditional classroom.

The latter type of experiential encounter proceeds through comprehension. It is realized through abstract conceptualization, whether via images or language. It occurs when the new swimmer's instructor says, "Let's look at five principles of swimming." The usual result is a single-sense experience appealing to the intellect. This cognition-oriented experience is the typical mode of formal classroom settings. Kolb's point here is not to denigrate one type of prehension beneath another. Apprehension and comprehension are both important elements of a learning process. A robust learning theory acknowledges the validity of both modes and the necessity of helping students encounter experience in both ways.

Just as there are two ways of encountering experience, so too are there two ways of transforming experience: reflective observation or active experimentation. Learning does not occur simply by encountering a stream of experience, whether through apprehension or comprehension. Rather, that encounter with experience must be transformed, either by reflective observation, a process Kolb calls "intention," or by active experimentation, a process referred to as "extension." Reflective observation occurs as a new experience interacts with past individual experience or personal knowledge. Without reflection, apprehension of concrete experience amounts to only a stream of sensory stimulation, with no learning actually taking place. Likewise, without reflective observation, comprehended experience sits as an island of abstraction, never connected to the learner's existing knowledge. The process of reflection integrates new experiences into existing knowledge so that new knowledge is created. Figure 3.1 illustrates how

---

10. I am using the word "encounter" as a label for Kolb's term "prehension dimension." Kolb describes this dimension as the means of grasping experience.

reflective observation is positioned as a transformative agent for appre-
hended experience and comprehended experience.

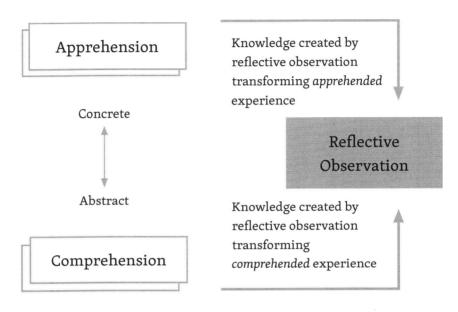

FIGURE 3.1. Learning through Reflective Observation

An alternative mode of transforming experience occurs through active
experimentation. As implied in the name, the learner extends an experience
(whether that experience came by apprehension or by comprehension)
through a new trial. This reaction or experiment modifies in some way the
original sense gained through the experience. The learner transforms a
new experience with a "let's-try-this" reaction, thereby creating knowledge.

When the two types of encountering experience (apprehension and
comprehension) are combined with the two types of transforming experience (reflective observation and active experimentation), four potential
ways of learning may be discovered.[11] By way of illustration, return to the

---

11. Preferences for learning one way over another are explored elsewhere as "learning
styles."

example of learning to swim. First comes an experience encounter. The learner may gain a new experience through a concrete experience of jumping into the water (apprehension). Alternatively, our swimming novice may gain experience through an abstract conceptualization of receiving verbal instruction about how to swim (comprehension). As noted earlier, these experiences in and of themselves do not constitute learning. Rather, they must be transformed. Engaging in reflective observation, our learner may choose to reflect on the concrete experience of sinking into water with arms flailing wildly and draw conclusions about the nature of swimming. Or this learner may also have drawn conclusions through reflection, transforming comprehended experience about swimming. In a similar fashion, an individual learning to swim might be engaged in a concrete experience of sinking in water and choose to transform that experience through active experimentation. In this instance, the learner may well modify movements of arms and feet to try to prevent drowning. Kolb argues that learning occurs best as we integrate the four combinations of experiences plus transformations. Figure 3.2 illustrates how apprehension and comprehension are related to the transformative process of active experimentation.

IMPLICATIONS FOR TEACHING HOMILETICS

Experiential learning theory provides a robust framework from which to draw several implications for teaching homiletics. However, in the interest of brevity, I will posit only a few ideas for the homiletics classroom, dividing my comments between the professor's role and the student's role.

Those who seek to use experiential learning theory in teaching homiletics must think of education less as depositing knowledge into students' minds and more as designing and executing learning experiences that will help students create knowledge. Experiential learning theory validates heavy reliance on lab experiences where students engage in the concrete experience of preaching. However, preaching in a lab may not be viewed as a test. It is not primarily an assessment of what the student has learned. Rather, the preaching lab is where concrete experience is encountered. The learning and the doing cannot be separated easily. Like being thrown into the pool to learn how to swim, standing to preach to peers provides a multi-sensory encounter that provides the basis for creating knowledge.

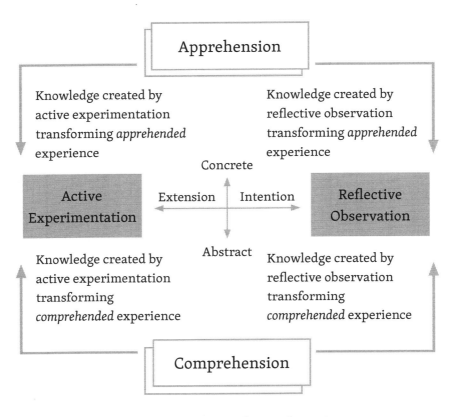

FIGURE 3.2. Four Potential Ways of Learning

The lab experience by itself, however, does not constitute learning. Students must be given opportunity to reflect on their experience, thereby transforming the experience and creating knowledge. This reflection may be enhanced by feedback from the professor and other students. Throughout this reflective observation, students are connecting their newest experiences with previously held ideas, experiences, attitudes, etc. Of course, a professor will design other learning experiences (such as reading a book about preaching) whereby students will have opportunity to engage in abstract conceptualization. This may include discussion about course readings, other sermons, and course notes. While students may be helped with concepts given directly by a professor, they may experience even greater learning if they derive and articulate concepts through their own thinking processes (whether on their own or in community).

Finally, the professor will want to provide space whereby students may actively experiment with their ideas about preaching. Such experimentation may be incorporated into class time or encouraged in real-life settings outside of class. Regardless of the venue for experimentation, professors will want to encourage students to experiment and then value the resulting transformations such experiments may have on the student's original concrete experience or on their abstract conceptualizations. Professors who engage in such activities will see themselves not primarily as dispensers of knowledge (as subject matter experts) but as learning coaches whose design of experiences charts a pathway for students to learn how to preach. Further, they will not settle for just one or two ways of stimulating creation of knowledge. Rather, they will seek to use multiple ways to help students learn and affirm the individual creation of knowledge about preaching. In other words, professors may need to adjust their expectations about the degree of uniformity expected from students, both in terms of outcomes and in terms of learning processes. Not all students will learn via the same pathway, a reality to embrace rather than meet with regret.

In sum, professors could answer the following questions about the design of their homiletics courses:

1. At what points in my courses do students encounter concrete preaching experience? (Lab? Field?)

2. At what points in my courses do students encounter abstract conceptualization about preaching? (Readings? Lectures? Recordings?)

3. Where does my course stimulate students' reflective observation on the concrete and abstract experiences encountered? (Written reflections? Dialogue? Discussions?)

4. Where does the course provide opportunity for students to engage in active experimentation? (Lab? Field? Redesign?)

As for students engaged in experiential learning, they also take on a new role. Rather than simply expecting a professor to tell them how to preach, students take an active role in their own learning and in each other's learning. They don't come to a course expecting to acquire the notes or extract knowledge from the mind of the professor; rather, they come expecting to take responsibility to engage new learning experiences,[12] and in some cases even design the learning experiences themselves. They make plans to reflect on their experiences and experiment in ways that they themselves initiate. Along the way, they learn how to help one another reflect, comprehend, and experiment with preaching concepts and skills.[13] I personally have countless experiences of students offering positive, helpful critique to other students as they prepare and deliver sermons. When students engage in self critique as well as peer critique, the learning process is enhanced and students walk away with a feeling of empowerment.

Experiential learning theory challenges those who teach preaching to craft learning experiences for their students and provide opportunities for students to transform those experiences into personal knowledge. Preaching labs can be instrumental in this quest, but only if labs are linked to transformative processes that use reflection and experimentation. In classrooms whose instructors seek to use experiential learning theory, the roles of professor and students will need to be redefined so that responsibilities are properly positioned to stimulate creation of knowledge.

And one of the best ways to capitalize on experiential learning theory is through the use of dialogue.

HOW DOES DIALOGUE INFLUENCE
THE LEARNING OF HOMILETICS?

At United States Bible colleges and seminaries, it is not unusual for professors to engage students in dialogue.[14] It is all part of developing a nice, friendly Christian community. Professors frequently share life with students, often in some effort to serve as mentor, quasi-mentor, or advisor. Yet

---

12. One of the ways I have helped students take responsibility for their own learning is to challenge them to produce the course notes. Rather than have notes handed out from the professor, students summarize readings and class discussions. These course notes are then extended to launch new interactions and stimulate learning in ways I did not originally anticipate at the start of the course.

13. Jerome Bruner speaks of learners "scaffolding" one another, an apt metaphor for the idea that students support one another in the learning process so that professors do not monopolize the teacher role. See Bruner, *The Culture of Education*, 21.

14. Dialogue between teachers and students is not a normal occurrence in other parts of the world. In parts of Africa and Asia, cultural norms dictate that that teachers not be approached by students to engage in conversation.

this kind of dialogue tends to be positioned as extra-curricular. It is pursued outside of the classroom, for the classroom is reserved as a space for dissemination of information. Such relationship-enhancing dialogue may occur in hallways and during office hours. But what if dialogue was much more important to the whole process of learning? What if dialogue is not ancillary to education but critical to it? Indeed, this section of the chapter advances the idea that dialogue should be pursued as integral to education.

Learning to Listen, Learning to Teach is Jane Vella's primary publication in which she advocates for the pursuit of dialogue in education.[15] Drawing on the works of Freire, Knowles, Jung, Lewin, and others, Vella positions her work more as a practitioner than a theorist. However, she clearly seeks to advance the ideas of these educational theorists, particularly in helping educators apply adult learning theory and experiential learning theory through dialogue in education.

The title of Vella's book, Learning to Listen, Learning to Teach, indicates the position taken therein: one learns to teach by learning to listen to students. It is in this dialogue that students truly learn best. Or connecting Vella's thesis to experiential learning vernacular: *students excel in creating knowledge when they are engaged in dialogue.*

Rather than give extensive defense for the use of dialogue, Vella's work primarily sets forth principles that help educators practice dialogue education. Before proceeding to selected principles from Vella, consider first three benefits of dialogue to the concept of experiential learning developed in the previous section.

First, dialogue can be an arena for both encountering and transforming experience. Dialogue itself can be a concrete experience (apprehension) in which the dynamics of conversation provide sensations that would not occur in less personal interaction. More likely, dialogue enhances abstract conceptualization (comprehension) as students tune their own articulations of concepts that are taking shape in their minds. A community of negotiation develops in which individuals negotiate the meaning of concepts. Perhaps more directly, dialogue becomes a pathway for reflective observation. Students foreground the interaction of their past learning

---

15. Jane Vella, Learning to Listen, Learning to Teach: The Power of Dialogue in Educating Adults, rev. ed. (San Francisco: Jossey Bass, 2002).

or experiences with a new experience under consideration. Dialogue has the potential to make reflection overt, increasing the benefit explicit for the entire community of learners. Finally, think of dialogue as a form of active experimentation, as learners float new ideas and test out their tentative hypotheses in a verbal arena.

Beyond thinking of dialogue as an arena for encountering and transforming experience, consider it as a bridge to experiences from one person to another. It is through dialogue that teachers learn enough about students to design meaningful learning experiences for a course. Further, teachers adapt learning experiences to learners through dialogue, and it is through dialogue that learners inform teachers about the progress of these learning experiences. As students engage in dialogue with one another, they connect their experiences and their creation of knowledge. In the dialogical process, additional knowledge is then created. In the end, dialogue is the fuel to creating knowledge because it is a bridge from experiences to experiences.

A third benefit of dialogue education is that it empowers students. While this benefit is not directly linked to Kolb's discussion of experiential learning, the empowering nature of dialogue is a significant benefit. Critical educators such as Paulo Freire[16] and Henry Giroux[17] have brought to our attention the oppressive nature of much schooling, an oppression that is carried out by course design and by pedagogy. The single voice (monologue) of a teacher sounding out from a single perspective is unlikely to avoid subjecting students to a single view of reality. True dialogue, however, providing students a space to establish their voices, potentially empowers students, and engenders a sense of self-esteem in regard to thinking and learning. By "true" dialogue, I am referring not to closed-ended questions that cajole students for answers deemed right by the teacher; rather, I am referring to dialogue in which the student's perspective is truly valued and affirmed.[18] In his book on theological education, Reuel Howe explains how a teacher who directly answers questions promotes dependency rather

---

16. Freire, *Pedagogy of the Oppressed*.

17. Henry A. Giroux, *Pedagogy and the Politics of Hope: Theory, Culture, and Schooling* (Boulder, CO: Westview Press, 1997).

18. This is not to say that there is a neat delineation between monologue/lecture and dialogue/discussion. Burbules and Bruce provide an extensive analysis of the dichotomy,

than empowering of students in their abilities to ask questions and work toward answers. He states:

> When a question is put to an authority, he often answers what is being asked instead of using his knowledge, understanding, and skill to help his inquirers move in the direction of finding answers to their own questions. ... He has not discovered the greater excitement and satisfaction of having learners experience for themselves, with guidance, of course, the joy of acquiring insight and knowledge. Because teachers so often rush to give their own answers and opinions to questions, instead of using their resources to help others learn, much that passes for education weakens the student rather than strengthens him, and makes him more dependent rather than more resourceful. This has been the effect of much theological education and candidates for the ministry during their training period.[19]

How can teachers of preaching incur the benefits mentioned here? It is far from easy.[20] Yet Vella contends that adults can be in conversation with any teacher on any subject and it is dialogue that enables them to create learning from life's experiences. The remainder of her book provides principles for engaging students in dialogue. A few of those principles are listed next.

---

examining the issue from the stance of discourse analysis. They state, "As a result of such considerations, any useful theoretical frame will need to move beyond the simple, dichotomous monologue/dialogue distinction to, at the very least, a spectrum along which various pedagogical communicative relations can be classified from the relatively univocal and directive to the relatively reciprocal and open-ended. From this perspective, some things that look like lectures might be in fact quite 'dialogical'; while things that look like dialogues might be highly directive and narrow. Here, again, we need to move beyond 'speech act' analyses (who speaks, how much they speak, etc.) to look at the discursive content and how it is heard and responded to by others. Despite the etymologies of 'monologue' and 'dialogue,' the idea that all we have to do is count how many people are speaking in order to settle the pedagogical question appears quite crude and unhelpful." Nicholas C. Burbules and Bertram C. Bruce, "Theory and Research on Teaching as Dialogue," http://faculty.education.illinois.edu/burbules/papers/dialogue.html.

19. Reuel L. Howe, *The Miracle of Dialogue* (San Francisco: Harper, 1993), 52.

20. Professors find dialogue difficult because their own education usually did not provide them with good models. Further, students initially find dialogue difficult because they have fallen under the powerful negative influence of excessive use of electronic communication and social media. For a fascinating study of this dynamic, see Sherry Turkle, *Reclaiming Conversation: The Power of Talk in a Digital Age* (New York: Penguin Press, 2015).

NEEDS ASSESSMENT

Vella advocates thorough needs-assessment of students so that teachers might design learning experiences that are fitted to the students. Such assessments help the teacher understand existing learning levels, concerns, and even what students really want to learn. By isolating students' wants and needs, an educator can have confidence that the course design will be acceptable to students because it targets what they value. The assessment of needs begins well before the course and continues as the course progresses.

Homileticians ought to be quick to act on this idea, for most would not think of preaching sermons that are unrelated to the felt needs of an audience. Yet somehow the idea of connecting student needs to course design may have escaped us. Rather than be shaped by a professor's notes or the table of contents in a book (which may be extremely logical), professors would do well to proceed through a course based on listening to student need. Most students come to their first preaching course as people who have heard many sermons. They already have some idea of the characteristics of good and bad sermons. They know what it means to be clear and what it means to be relevant. They likely have some ideas about the importance of clarity and relevance. A needs-based approach to education will not repeat definitions or cast a vision for clarity or relevance if students already have that knowledge as part of their experience. On the other hand, some groups of students may be so pessimistic about preaching that they need a professor to help them catch a vision for how to preach effectively. Likewise, a professor would be wise to know if students are afraid of preaching. If so, why? Do they feel preaching is important, or are they simply in the class because it is required for their degree? Do they come from a particular denomination that specifies what acceptable preaching is? Answers to these questions influence what is taught and how it is taught. It is fascinating to watch what happens when teachers of homiletics adjust course design to meet students' needs, rather than teach to a set curriculum that may appear to be distant from felt student needs. As Vella says, "Motivation is magically enhanced, however, when we teach them about their own themes. People are naturally excited to learn anything that helps them understand their own themes, their own lives."[21]

---

21. Vella, *Learning to Listen, Learning to Teach*, 6.

SAFETY AND SOUND RELATIONSHIPS

I am here combining two of Vella's principles because, while they are different, they both affect student perception and how well they will pursue creation of knowledge. First, students must have a sense of safety in the classroom, that is, a sense that they truly will have success in achieving the learning that they want to do. Their perspective on the course is characterized not by fear but by confidence, for they see the plan and believe they can accomplish the learning experiences set before them. A sense of safety develops when students feel they are starting with tasks that they can successfully do before moving to difficult and complex iterations. Additionally, students feel safe when the learning atmosphere is nonjudgmental and assuring. Vella underlines the importance of safety with the following statement:

> Affirmation of every offering from every learner, as well as lavish affirmation of efforts and products of learning tasks, can create a sense of safety that invites creativity and spontaneity in dealing with new concepts, skills, and attitudes. Affirming is one of the basic tasks of every teacher.[22]

While safety deals primarily with a student's confidence in the course design, the principle of sound relationships focuses on the relationship between students and teachers. Professors must recognize that the power disparity between professor and student can be a significant detriment to learning. Students are afraid to speak, experiment, or ask questions when the professor may be displeased by any of these things or wields power against the student in expression of that displeasure. Professors who are serious about creating sound relationships will work hard to listen and will be humble about their own knowledge and experience. Without sound relationships, dialogue will not fully develop.

Teachers of homiletics cannot assume that because their classroom is in a Bible college or seminary that principles of safety and sound relationships are automatically met. Some students fear standing in front of an audience—especially an audience made up of their peers and a professor. Most will dread the idea of speaking without notes (or with minimal

---

22. Vella, *Learning to Listen, Learning to Teach*, 10.

notes). Others will simply hate preaching because they do not believe they have the "gift" and so will not succeed in the class. Still others will view the professor as such an exalted authority that they dare not raise questions that loom important for their own learning. As a result, those who teach preaching must make every effort to give students a sense of safety in the class and an assurance that professorial power will not be used to belittle or embarrass the student. While students must receive substantial critique of their sermons, it must be done with sensitivity so that they feel affirmed. Of course, this ratio of critique to affirmation varies by student, so it is incumbent on the professor to know each student well enough to gauge the effects of critique and the need for affirmation. I have personally found that having students in my home for a casual meal is the single most influential activity that helps develop sound relationships between students as well as between professor and students. With sound relationships established, affirmations are embraced by students and critique is heard without the cutting effect that might otherwise occur. A professor who can be perceived as parent, coach, and friend is more likely to be heard and to be asked deep questions from students than the professor who is viewed only as expert and critic. Students must believe that their teacher really does want them to succeed in the class and beyond.

SEQUENCE AND REINFORCEMENT

While Vella's principle related to safety (above) introduced the concept of sequence, it here receives its own emphasis. The sequence of learning tasks needs to be from easy to difficult, from simple to complex, and from group-supported to solo efforts. It is only through dialogue that a teacher can know if students are perceiving the sequence of activities positively. Further, professors must be willing to alter course sequence when they discover that students are fearful about moving forward. Obviously, this means that the initial course schedule or syllabus must move from status of master to servant. Vella explains how proper sequence is indicated in the response of students:

> Manifestations of safety and enthusiasm and readiness to achieve in learners indicate that sequence is being honored. When you, as teacher, see fear, confusion, and reluctance to try in the learner,

test the sequence of the learning task. You may find you have not honored their need for small steps between tasks and their need for reinforcement.[23]

Sequence is particularly challenging for the process of teaching preaching, as preaching is a complex task built on several prerequisite skills. Further, two groups of preaching students could have vastly different levels of these prerequisite skills. Professors must be willing to listen to students and adjust sequence as needed. For example, let's say that several students in a first-year preaching course have had no public speaking experience, and that lack of experience has manifested into significant fear at the prospect of delivering their first sermon. The professor seeking to honor the concept of sequence will try to find a way to give these students a positive public speaking experience that is easier and less threatening than a full sermon.

In many cases, professors of preaching face particularly difficult questions about sequence. For example, course objectives may include preaching sermons that are true to the text, clear, interesting, and relevant. Can this be learned in sequence? In some sense, all these features need to be present in all sermons. Perhaps teachers of preaching can develop levels of proficiency in each of these areas so that the sequence gives students confidence in the course design.

Related to the concept of sequence is that of reinforcement. Reinforcement involves reiterating concepts and skills so that they are learned thoroughly. I have found that reinforcement is most effective when students are given opportunity in dialogue to restate what they have learned in the course. When done frequently, such as rebuilding course concepts, students are assured they really are accomplishing course objectives. Teachers of preaching struggle taking time for reinforcement as there is always a new concept to cover in a course. However, the best course designs have reinforcement built into them. More learning can often be accomplished with less content.

Vella provides a total of twelve principles. While all have value, the four discussed above are those that seem to be most directly applicable to the teaching of homiletics. Application of the principles encourages dialogue

---

23. Vela, *Learning to Listen, Learning to Teach*, 13.

and is produced as the result of dialogue. Of course, the value in all of this is the recognition that dialogue connects directly to students' experience and is thus integral to the process of creating knowledge through the transformation of experience.

Learning is thus a process whereby knowledge is created through the transformation of experience with dialogue being a vital link to experience, for both teachers and students. This requires that professors value needs assessment, safety, sound relationships, sequence, and reinforcement.

However, there is another dynamic that affects students' learning.

HOW DOES THE CULTURE OF EDUCATION AFFECT THE TEACHING AND LEARNING OF HOMILETICS?

Since teachers of preaching regularly think about their audiences, they most likely have developed a sensitivity to culture. They may be aware they have students in their classes from different cultures. And they may recognize they are training students to serve people in different cultures. While such sensitivities have their own bearing on education, the focus of this section is on a different kind of cultural dynamic, namely, the interaction between culture and education. At issue is how the school itself is situated in culture and often fails to identify how that prevailing culture affects the design and execution of education. This culture in which the school lives makes authoritative demands upon the school, pressuring schools to comply with its expectations.

In *Culture of Education*, Jerome Bruner investigates the interplay between schooling and culture. The main idea of his work is that education "is a complex pursuit of fitting a culture to the needs of its members and of fitting its members and their ways of knowing to the needs of the culture."[24] Bruner provides not so much a theory as a set of ideas to help us see elements of this interaction so that we might design our schools, curricula, and teaching methods with conscious awareness of the forces working on us and of the inertia resisting our graduates as we send them out into that culture. In effect, he issues a call to educators to see how schools are situated in culture and impacted by them. He calls this a "culturalist" approach to education.

---

24. Bruner, *The Culture of Education*, 43.

To help educators take a culturalist approach to education, Bruner begins by contrasting culturalist and computational views of mind. The latter view sees the mind much like a computer; it excels at information processing. Such a view of the mind works well when information is clearly definable, unambiguous, and decontextualized. (The statement "2 + 2 = 4" is influenced little by cultural constraints and pressures.) A computational view of the mind serves us well when we know the information that needs to be "looked up" in the mind's registers. In this framework, teaching is a process whereby information is organized and fed to the mind so that it might be stored, recalled, and used as needed.

In contrast to the computational view, a culturalist view of the mind sees learning as a quest for meaning-making, and this quest is inseparably tied to culture. Indeed, culture provides the symbol system (namely, language) by which the meaning-making process moves forward. Culture establishes the source of meaning and the significance accorded to ideas, skills, etc. This culturalist view of the mind affirms that meaning-making is filled with ambiguity. It is a messy project, characterized by perspective and negotiation. It cannot be separated from language or value. Learning is essentially a hermeneutical process, and the quest to learn is a journey into intersubjectivity—that is, how humans come to know each other's minds.

While the preceding description is necessarily abstract, it raises several issues about teaching homiletics. First, how do teachers of homiletics view minds? If the mind is more like a computational device (a conception particularly appealing for those positively oriented toward the culture of science), then curriculum and teaching methods will reflect an information-processing model. Indeed, preaching itself would be conceived of as a method of gaining information from the Bible and directing it effectively to an audience. Preachers analyze biblical information with exegetical tools and shape their messages according to rules of sermon design. The sermon would then be delivered according to rules about effective public speaking and communication dynamics. Notice the emphasis on rules and methods in the three preceding sentences. Such an emphasis characterizes a computational view of mind. One might almost think that a computer with sufficient artificial intelligence could be programmed to handle the tasks of exegesis, sermon design, and sermon delivery.

A teacher holding a culturalist view of the mind might engage in a rather different conception of preaching and of pedagogy, beginning with the recognition that education is occurring amid the culture of the church. This church culture has significant bearing on how one views preachers and the process of preaching. The Bible alone does not define the content of sermons or acceptable means of sermon delivery. Bruner and other similar theorists would have us recognize that whether or not the educator is conscious of this reality, culture (in our case church culture) is in fact providing us with the very conceptions of what we seek to teach. We are always, at least to some degree, relying on the toolkit of culture to equip us with the stuff of education. Education is, whether we recognize it or not, a transmission of culture with the meanings and significance supplied by that culture.[25]

By way of illustration, consider how the differences in three church cultures might influence the concept of "true to the text." An individual with a computational view of mind might consider a sermon idea to be true to the text if it meets a set of rules (lexicography, semantical, syntactical, etc.) for validating exegesis. Now consider three different preachers who take a culturalist approach to preaching and to education. Those who teach preaching for an evangelical church context might conceive of an idea as true to the text only if the veracity is established from several proofs from biblical texts. A teacher of preaching for a high church context might be unwilling to consider an idea as true to the text unless the biblical support is coupled with church teaching or church tradition. A teacher for a Pentecostal context might consider an idea to be true to the text only if it is delivered by an individual who clearly has a prophetic voice. Thus, a value like being true to the text does not fit well into a computational view of the mind (though it might be taught that way) and will have meaning variously negotiated based on cultural context. To teach a student to be true to the text is a hermeneutical (meaning-making) endeavor.

---

25. Since at least the 1950s, anthropologists and ethnographers have studied how education is the transmission of culture. For a helpful review of the history of the anthropology of education, see the compilation by George Spindler, ed., *Education and Cultural Process: Anthropological Approaches*, 2nd ed. (Prospects Heights, IL: Waveland Press, 1987). Of course, ethnographers and anthropologists take a descriptive approach to the relationship between education and culture, while critical theorists (Freire, Giroux, etc.) are particularly concerned about the oppressive impacts of culture that may well be undetected by most educators.

Bruner amplifies this basic idea through a discussion of his "perspectival tenet." He writes, "The meaning of any fact, proposition, or encounter is relative to the perspective or frame of reference in terms of which it is construed."[26] Clearly, it is important for learners to have some idea of alternative meanings of a term or idea to better understand the concept under consideration. The issue is not agreement with the other perspectives, but awareness of the perspectives and an ability to see and appreciate what the other perspectives may add to the idea under scrutiny. Indeed, the American court system works along this same set of assumptions. Take, for example, a jury "learning" about a car-pedestrian accident. At issue is the meaning of the statement "the car and the pedestrian collided." To determine what that statement means (and establish fault, or significance), the court will hear from multiple witnesses, gaining various perspectives. From one side of the street, a witness has the perspective that the driver failed to stop her car and therefore hit the pedestrian. From another side of the street, a witness declares that the pedestrian stepped into the path of the car. A mechanic, upon inspection of the car, offers the perspective that the car's brakes were not functioning properly. Multiple perspectives could all be true and all important for establishing the meaning of the statement "the car and the pedestrian collided." While we might appreciate the multi-perspective view of reality in the court, it may be unappreciated in the classroom, especially if the professor's perspective is the only one that matters or if dialogue is suppressed so that student perspectives are never given voice.

Evangelicals may grow nervous with the idea that multiple perspectives are at play in establishing reality. The basic modernist assumption is that reality is discovered rather than created through perception. But Bruner is quick to point out that a perspectival tenet for education does not mean every perspective is equally valid. This is not necessarily a step down a slippery path of inevitable relativism. Note Bruner's concise defense:

> Understanding in any one particular way is only "right" or "wrong" from the particular perspective in terms of which it is pursued. But the "rightness" of particular interpretations, while dependent on

---

26. Bruner, *The Culture of Education*, 13.

perspectives, also reflects rules of evidence, consistency, and coherence. Not everything goes. There are inherent criteria of rightness, and the possibility of alternative interpretations does not license all of them equally. A perspectival view of meaning making does *not* preclude common sense or "logic."[27]

The teacher of homiletics comes to grip with the perspectival nature of learning at the moment of trying to define "preach" or "preacher." A professor who highly esteems his own subject matter expertise is likely to provide a non-negotiable definition for students. This is presented as the "right" way to view preaching and will of necessity be reproduced by students on an exam. However, what if we do not have the final word on this matter? Whether a professor acknowledges it or not, students will create their own knowledge about what constitutes preaching. They will have different perspectives. Perhaps a more effective (not to mention humbler) approach to education is to help students articulate their perspectives, guide them, affirm them, and set them on a lifelong journey of finding the meanings of "preach" and "preacher." So, we put students on a trajectory of learning, not just in development of skills but also in making meaning of the various concepts of the discipline.[28]

A culturalist approach to education acknowledges the interplay of professorial perspective, student perspective, and the perspective of a broader culture in which the school is situated. The recognition of these three elements means that education lives in tension between accommodating cultures and changing them. Bruner explains this risk:

An effective educational enterprise lives in the tension between transmitting the culture deemed appropriate by its sponsoring communities/stakeholders and developing in the students a different version of the world. This is a high-risk situation. Err on the

---

27. Bruner, *The Culture of Education*, 14. For additional insight into the roles of fidelity and coherence in establishing reality, see Walter R. Fisher, *Human Communication as Narration: Toward a Philosophy of Reason, Value, and Action* (Columbia: University of South Carolina, 1989).

28. When professors refuse to give students this kind of freedom, they run the risk of producing students who, at a later time in their lives, will feel guilty when they move away from the professor's definitions. So, the unintended result is suppression of lifelong learning rather than stimulating it.

transmission side, and we only exacerbate the problems of the day. Err on the side of revolution, and we lose acceptance with the very communities we desire to reach.[29]

It is incumbent upon professors of preaching to listen to student perspectives. They must know something of the challenge of fitting students to the culture (preparing students for the church) and how much they can push back against that culture with revolutionary or idealistic teachings (sending out students as instruments of change).

Closely related to this discussion is the recognition that education always deeply affects identity and self-esteem. Bruner points out that public schools traditionally have not done well with designing education to help students develop their sense of agency.[30] That is, schools subconsciously negatively affect a student's sense that she can originate and carry out activity in the culture. Further, Bruner would have us consider how self-esteem is developed through one's sense they will fit into the culture in a meaningful way and positively impact that culture. When a student's school experience is riddled with failure, it is unlikely that a high self-esteem will result. A resulting question for educators is how well their classes develop a healthy sense of self for students, giving them a proper recognition of who they are with an ability to overcome fears about what they will become.

Students of preaching may well face a greater affront to their concept of self than in other courses. Their shortcomings are public. The critique they receive could deeply impact their concept of self, more than a score on their last written paper. And for many students, poor performance in preaching class may lead to deep personal questions about their fit for ministry, their effectiveness in serving the Lord, and even their ability to continue in theological education. Sometimes the students who have excelled in traditional research-oriented, paper-writing courses are those who will incur greatest damage to their concept of self in preaching courses. Professors of preaching will need to engage in dialogue with students to determine how their words might properly build self-esteem. This esteem-building

---

29. Bruner, *The Culture of Education*, 14.
30. Bruner, *The Culture of Education*, 35–37.

feedback will not be the same for every student. Further, as discussed earlier, sequence of learning experiences can provide a series of successes for students so that they walk away from each learning experience with a greater sense of progress, not only in a skill but in their own concept of self.

CONCLUSION

Professors of preaching are positioned to facilitate much learning in their students. The temptation might be to give students more books to read, more notes to store, and more research to complete. While books, notes, and research undoubtedly have their place, they are not optimally effective when they cause professors and students to focus on subject matter acquisition rather than on learning as a process.

This chapter calls professors of preaching to consider three theoretical bases to improve the design and execution of their courses. The core idea is a challenge to think of learning as a process (rather than a set of outcomes) whereby knowledge is created (rather than simply acquired) through the transformation of experience. Connections to experience occur principally through dialogue—that is, professor-to-student dialogue and student-to-student dialogue. This opens up a culturalist view of education, one that recognizes the interplay between schooling and culture. These broad strokes of theory can lead to a wide variety of teaching methods. If you are willing to explore such methods, you will create knowledge not only for yourself but for a whole community of learners in the profession.

4

o o o

Teach so Students Can Learn:
Teaching Preaching and Learning Styles

JOHN V. TORNFELT

Teaching, on its own, never causes learning. Only successful
attempts by the learner to learn causes learning.[1]

How is it that a new professor of preaching can meaningfully influence the thinking of a few students but not the rest of the class? Why does another instructor lead a group to become skilled practitioners but fails to connect with the rest of the class? The reason is often apparent: as well intentioned as professors may be, they are unschooled in the dynamics of learning.

In preparing men and women for positions in higher education, schools offer workshops on course design, pedagogy (not andragogy), selecting and organizing content, motivation, and evaluation. While such topics are valuable, how much do upcoming (and well-seasoned) professors know about teaching and learning? Maryellen Weimer writes: "The how-to-teach literature focuses attention almost exclusively on actions that teachers perform. That effective teaching results in learning is assumed but rarely discussed explicitly. The preoccupation of the pedagogical literature provides clear evidence of a profession tightly connected to teaching but only loosely linked to learning."[2] Hence, there is a considerable need for a greater awareness of learning styles.

Learning styles describe the ways in which people gather, interpret, organize, and assimilate facts before coming to conclusions. While

---

1. Grant Wiggins and Jay McTighe, *Understanding by Design*, 2nd ed. (Upper Saddle River, NJ: Pearson Education, 2005), 228.

2. Maryellen Weimer, *Learner-Centered Teaching* (San Francisco: Jossey-Bass, 2002), 73.

definitions are numerous, each conveys a belief that the potential of students to learn is "effectively and easily (enhanced) if the instruction is tailored to their individual styles."[3]

Sensitivity to learning is not a new concept but can be traced to Augustine of Hippo (354–430) in his use of rhetorical principles in preaching. Beverly Zink-Sawyer writes:

> Augustine applied the devices of classical rhetoric to the proclamation of the gospel not for the ultimate goal of eloquence but to enable those who hear to be moved rather than taught, so that they may not be sluggish in putting what they know into practice and so that they may fully accept those things which they acknowledge to be true. Augustine suggested that the speaker-preacher be attentive to the listeners in order to discern the level of comprehension among them. Until the crowd shows by its motion whether it understands, and until it signifies comprehension, the matter being discussed should be expressed in a variety of ways.[4]

Understanding styles is not only pertinent for instructors, but students as well; awareness aids them in breaking out of their learning boxes. Stephen Brookfield writes: "Becoming aware of learning styles and learning how to adjust for weaknesses and emphasize strengths, is not a pedagogic exercise of interest only to academics. It is a fundamentally liberating way by which we can free ourselves of tendencies and inclinations that act to prevent us from becoming critical thinkers."[5]

To visualize the relationship of the traits of learning styles, Lynn Curry categorized and likened them to layers of an onion.[6] Subsequently, her

---

3. Harold Pashler et al., "Learning Styles: Concepts and Evidence," *Psychological Science in the Public Interest* 9:3 (2008): 107.

4. Beverly Zink-Sawyer, "The Word Purely Preached and Heard: The Listeners and the Homiletical Endeavor," *Interpretation* 51, no. 4 (1997): 351.

5. Stephen D. Brookfield, *Developing Critical Thinkers* (San Francisco: Jossey-Bass, 1987), 85.

6. Lynn Curry, "An Organization of Learning Styles Theory and Constructs" (paper presented at the annual meeting of the American Educational Research Association in Montreal, Quebec, April 1983).

model was expanded by Charles Claxton and Patricia Murrell to four levels and is depicted in figure 4.1.[7]

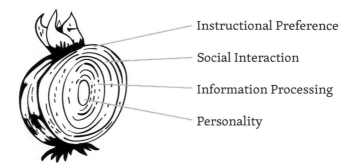

Instructional Preference

Social Interaction

Information Processing

Personality

FIGURE 4.1. Four Levels of Learning Styles

These levels are not discrete or self-contained but should be understood holistically. At the core is personality, which is the most predictable level and least subject to change. Moving outward, traits become less stable and susceptible to variation. Yet in moving toward the periphery, inner traits exert influence on the next layers. Hence, personality impacts the ability to process information, and social interaction tendencies inform instructional preferences.

But why concern ourselves with learning styles? Richard Felder and Linda Silverman's words are helpful, though their context pertains to engineering students:

> Mismatches exist between common learning styles of engineering students and traditional teaching styles of engineering professors. In consequence, students become bored and inattentive in class, do poorly on tests, get discouraged about the courses, the curriculum, and themselves, and in some cases change to other curricula or drop out of school. Professors, confronted by low test grades, unresponsive or hostile classes, poor attendance and dropouts, know

---

7. Charles Claxton and Patricia K. Murrell, "Learning Styles: Implications for Improving Educational Practice," ASHE-ERIC Higher Education Report No. 4, Washington, DC: Association for the Study of Higher Education (1987), 7.

something is not working; they may become overly critical of their students (making things even worse) or begin to wonder if they are in the right profession. Most seriously, society loses potentially excellent engineers.[8]

Substituting several words and phrases, their appraisal comparably applies to the students in our homiletics classes. It can be stated (italics mine):

> Mismatches exist between common learning styles of *seminarians* and the teaching style of their *professor of homiletics*. In consequence, students become bored or inattentive in class, do poorly *in preaching assignments*, get discouraged about *the seminary, church* and themselves and in some cases *pursue other types of ministries* or just drop out of school. Professors, confronted by *lackluster sermons,* know something is not working; they may become critical of students or begin to wonder if they are in the right *calling.* Most seriously, *churches* lose potential *communicators of the gospel (and the message of Christ is not proclaimed).*

PERSONALITY MODELS

At the core of learning styles is the personality of the learner. Representative models focus on people's deepest characteristics and how these traits shape their worldviews, impact how they manage tasks, and affect how they interact with people.

MYERS-BRIGGS TYPE INDICATOR

The Myers-Briggs Type Indicator (MBTI) stems from the work of Isabel Myers Briggs, who reconsidered Carl Jung's research on psychological types. This inventory identifies patterns used by people to take in information (perception) and make decisions (judging). It contends "the world can be perceived in two distinct ways—sensing or intuition—and people use two distinct and contrasting ways to reach conclusions or make

---

8. Richard M. Felder and Linda K. Silverman, "Learning and Teaching Styles in Engineering Education," *Engineering Education* 78, no. 7 (1988): 674.

judgments—thinking or feeling."[9] In addition to these preferences are the accompanying inclinations for extraversion or introversion and dispositions for either judging or perceiving.

The MBTI consists of four dichotomous scales and categories of people:

1. *Extroverts* (focus on the outer world of people, willingly try out new things) versus *introverts* (focus on the inner world of ideas and thinking through matters).

2. *Sensors* (practical, detail-oriented, factual, procedural) versus *intuitors* (conceptual, imaginative, interest in meanings and possibilities).

3. *Thinkers* (skeptical, decisions are logical and rule-oriented) versus *feelers* (appreciative, decisions are personal and considerate).

4. *Judgers* (set and follow agendas, seek closure even with incomplete information) versus *perceivers* (adapt with circumstances, resist closure to obtain more data).

HERRMANN'S BRAIN DOMINANCE MODEL

Ned Herrmann's model involves hemispheric dominance of the brain (often termed the right-brain/left-brain approach). The brain's left side is the seat of language and processes information in linear or sequential ways. Left-brain individuals are considered more logical in their processing. This hemisphere takes pieces of data and orderly arranges them before drawing conclusions. In contrast, the brain's right side is more visual, holistic, and innovative. Right-brain students process information more intuitively, emotively, randomly, and symbolically. They are inclined to see the larger picture before the details.[10]

---

9. Isabel Briggs Myers, with Peter Myers, *Gifts Differing* (Palo Alto, CA: Consulting Psychologist Press, 1995).

10. See Ned Herrmann, "The Creative Brain," *Training and Development Journal* 35, no. 10 (1981): 10–16.

IMPLICATIONS

Personality is a reflection of God's creative work. Though many factors impact personalities, people are essentially introverts or extroverts, thinkers or feelers, right- or left-brain, and analytical or relational. While traits may be dominant, rarely is anyone characterized by a single attribute but should be understood as being predisposed to it. Regardless, being created in God's image implies diversity should not only be accounted for but valued in our instruction.

However, this creational implication does not imply personality sets limitations on learning. Wilbert McKeachie writes, "Styles ... are not little boxes, neatly separated from one another; rather, they represent dimensions along which learners may differ. Each individual is unique, falling at different points along the various continua that the learning style inventories purport to measure."[11]

In other words, though everyone is fashioned with traits, it does not mean their styles are locked. Rather, personality indicates preferences and not limitations. Professors should perceive students as a multi-layered community, expect a variety of expressions of styles of learning, and account for them in class.

For example, extroverts readily participate in conversations and can be quick to ask questions. In contrast, introverts may be engaged in a discussion but passively absorbing the exchange and processing the ideas. Sensors value facts while intuitors are willing to think outside the box. Logical thinkers who like details sit alongside feelers who are sense-oriented. Thus, professors should use a wide variety of teaching strategies. They should know when it is time to lecture and when posing questions for group discussion is appropriate. Likewise, they should recognize when critiquing videos of excellent preachers is fitting and when students are ready to put principles into practice with in-class sermons.

Furthermore, the predispositions of hemispheric-learners are to be considered. Logical and sequential, left-brain learners appreciate a clear, detailed syllabus that includes program goals, course objectives, class assignments, and grading rubrics. Examples of exegetical and homiletical

---

11. Wilbert J. McKeachie, "Learning Styles Can Become Learning Strategies," *National Teaching and Learning Forum* 4, no. 6 (1995): 1–2.

outlines are to be included as well as manuscripts. In contrast, right-brain learners are not as inclined to attend to details and may "forget" to refer to the syllabus. So a well-developed document helps eliminate ambiguity and offers guidance for everyone.

INFORMATION-PROCESSING MODELS

Information-processing models consider what methods students use to engage their worlds. They reflect how people gather, sort, store, and utilize information to learn.

PASK'S APPROACH

Gordon Pask has identified two approaches to processing information: holistic and serialistic.[12] These strategies have been schematized as follows.[13]

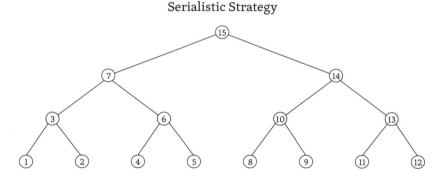

Serialistic Strategy

Note: Numbers relate to the sequence in which subtopics are learned.

FIGURE 4.2. Pask's Serialistic Information-Processing Model

---

12. See Gordon Pask, "Styles and Strategies of Learning," *British Journal of Educational Psychology*, 46 (1975): 128–48.

13. Nigel Ford, "Styles and Strategies for Processing Information: Implications for Professional Education," *Education for Information* 3 (1975): 3–15.

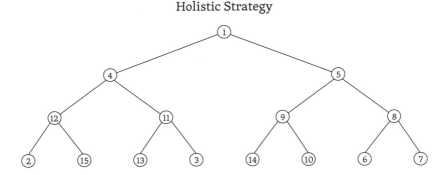

Note: Numbers relate to the sequence in which subtopics are learned.

FIGURE 4.3. Pask's Holistic Information-Processing Model

Serialists narrowly focus their attention on discrete pieces of information. Concerned with details and procedures, they prefer well-defined steps. They take a "bottom-up" approach, working slowly, logically, and thoroughly. These students are particular in following a prescribed pattern and are less likely to "skip around" while crafting a sermon.

More global in approach, holists use a broad framework. They look ahead, have a wider focus, and seek to build a "bigger picture" before determining where details fit.[14] In crafting a sermon, they are not as inclined to follow a format or "set of homiletical rules."

GREGORC'S STYLE DELINEATOR APPROACH

Anthony Gregorc has suggested learning styles emerge from people's natural predispositions and that they learn more efficiently from personal experience or abstract thinking.[15] He contends individuals perceive ideas in two ways: concrete-oriented (physical senses) or abstract-oriented (logical, deductive reasoning). Ordering enables individuals to organize their perceptions in sequential (systematic) or random (unorganized) ways. By

---

14. Ronald R. Schmeck, "Learning Styles of College Students," in Ronna F. Dillon and R. Schmeck, eds., *Individual Differences in Cognition* (New York: Academic Press, 1983), 236.

15. See Anthony F. Gregorc, *An Adult's Guide to Style* (Columbia, CT: Gregorc Associates, 1982).

crossing the dualities of concrete-abstract and random-sequential, four styles emerge as categorized by Cynthia Ulrich Tobias:[16]

Concrete Sequential	Abstract Sequential
hardworking	analytical
conventional	objective
accurate	knowledgeable
stable	thorough
dependable	structured
consistent	logical
factual	deliberate
organized	systematic

Abstract Random	Concrete Random
sensitive	quick
compassionate	intuitive
perceptive	curious
imaginative	realistic
idealistic	creative
sentimental	innovative
spontaneous	instinctive
flexible	adventurous

IMPLICATIONS

Robert Sternberg contends instructors are often ignorant of how students process information. He contends educators are "best at teaching people who match their own styles of thinking and learning ... [and] overestimate the extent to which students share their own styles."[17]

Serialistic and sequential learners prefer order to confusion and details rather than loose ends. A is followed by B, and B is followed by C. Only after the exegesis is complete are illustrations to be included and applications

16. Cynthia Ulrich Tobias, *The Way They Learn: How to Discover and Teach to Your Child's Strength* (Wheaton, IL: Tyndale House, 1994), 17.

17. Robert Sternberg, "Allowing for Thinking Styles," *Educational Leadership* 52, no. 3 (1994): 39.

made. To satisfy these well-organized and disciplined students, I give an extensive overview of my methodology in our first class. While I closely follow Haddon Robinson's ten stages of sermon development given in *Biblical Preaching*, I have added two additional stages: writing a manuscript and delivering the sermon. In that initial session, I give an extensive lecture to provide everyone a "mental map" of the content and process being covered during the semester.

In contrast, holistic learners are less systematic and may think of an introduction or illustration before finishing (or beginning) their exegetical work. While they may not construct their sermons "by the book," I accommodate their abstract and random styles and demonstrate how they can craft sermons that are still biblical and relevant. Visual learners appreciate my imaginary "homiletical wall." On the left side are the exegetical matters. To the right are contemporary and/or relational issues such as the introduction, illustrations, applications, and conclusion. I threaten (only humorously) students to not jump over this wall before completing their biblical research.

My wall model satisfies both learners by encouraging a spiraling between the exegetical and homiletical concerns. My approach is based on a belief that the mind is not able to make such precise distinctions between biblical and relational concerns.

Personally, I've used this model for years in crafting sermons. While analytical and sequential by nature, I frequently find myself stepping out of sequence when an illustration enters my mind. On countless occasions, an introduction has popped into my head during my initial reading of a text. While still having hermeneutical work to complete, I'm not quite able to ignore the insight. So, should I get ahead of myself, I am self-disciplined enough to know that I need to spiral back to the text and continue my research before moving ahead with illustrations and applications.

SOCIAL INTERACTION MODELS

These models consider how personal contacts and social settings impact learners' abilities to gather and utilize information.

GRASHA AND RIECHMANN-HRUSKA'S STUDENT
LEARNING STYLES

Grasha and Riechmann-Hruska have identified three styles of learning: avoidant-participant, competitive-collaborative, and dependent-independent. Subsequently, they integrated the styles with contextual dimensions (learner's attitudes toward the instruction, views of the teacher and/or peers, and reaction to procedures) to determine six styles:

1. *Independent* individuals like to think for themselves. Self-confident in their own abilities, they prefer working on their own, though they will listen to other people.

2. *Dependent* men and women have little intellectual curiosity and are willing to learn only what is required. Instructors are perceived as sources of structure and support and are looked to as authoritative figures.

3. *Collaborative* individuals enjoy learning within a group and view learning as a mutually enriching venture.

4. *Competitive* learners feel as if they are in a contest. Their reward for learning is doing better than other students. Consequently, the environment is understood as one in which they are to vie with individuals.

5. *Participant* individuals enjoy learning and see it as their responsibility to get as much as possible out of the situation (though they are not inclined to do what is required).

6. *Avoidant* men and women do not participate in learning and are not especially interested in the material.[18]

---

18. Anthony Grasha and Sheryl Riechmann-Hruska, "A Rational Approach to Developing and Assessing the Construct Validity of a Student Learning Style Scales Instrument," *Journal of Psychology* 87 (1974): 213–23.

Borrowing insights from the field of developmental psychology, Marcia Baxter Magolda has compared learning among college students as a function of their age, gender, and social expectations and has identified four stages of knowers:

1. *Absolute knowers* are common in the early years. Students believe teachers have the right answers and their responsibility is to get it right. They appreciate when a teacher makes the effort to be friendly and open.

2. *Transitional knowers* tend toward absolutist strategies. While they can be encouraged to experiment with different views, they want assurance of being correct.

3. *Independent knowers* are comfortable with understandings being open to various interpretations. They value instructors who promote independent thinking and willingness to exchange opinions.

4. *Contextual knowers* are comfortable critiquing their own knowledge and applying it to new or different contexts.[19]

IMPLICATIONS FOR PREACHING

Effective teaching flows naturally from relationships. If students have a sense of belonging, their engagement and motivation improve. Conversely, if feeling an aloofness or detachment, participation levels drop. But how does a professor create a positive environment?

My practice has been to walk around the classroom so as to get acquainted with the students. In our first meeting, I take the lead by sharing from my own journey (and seek to include a not-so-memorable preaching moment). Students should know I'm not a model of homiletical perfection but a fellow journeyman. As we continue around the room with introductions, I gather a sense of their personalities and expectations

---

19. See Marcia Baxter Magolda, *Knowing and Reasoning in College: Gender-Related Patterns in Students' Intellectual Development* (San Francisco: Jossey-Bass, 1992).

for the course, as well as fears or trepidations about preaching. Hopefully, this begins to establish a climate of trust that I can work to develop in the coming weeks. This is especially important as students prepare to preach in class. I want them to feel safe and believe, as David Lose writes, that "the instructor and peers offer critical input on their performance because they want the [student] to improve."[20]

I have also used small groups for reflective interactions. I have students organize themselves in groups (with the expectation of everyone participating) to work in round-table fashion on their sermons. This strategy is especially helpful as students ready themselves for their in-class sermons. One week before preaching, everyone is required to submit exegetical and homiletical outlines. Students offer and receive constructive criticism from group members. In so doing, students are not only receiving assistance but reinforcing what has already been covered in class.

Finally, I encourage students desiring additional input to submit their sermons for my feedback. While not all learners are inclined to ask, dependent and competitive students appreciate my input. Occasionally, process-oriented students will ask for a second look, and I am glad to help out. Such individuals are eager to learn and benefit when extra attention is given.

INSTRUCTIONAL PREFERENCE

The onion's outermost layer deals with students' instructional preferences. As discussed, it is important that a professor's instructional bent correspond as much as possible with that of the students. But how? It can be extremely challenging because of the diversity of styles found in any classroom. I can hear professors asking, with a degree of frustration in their voices, "How can I teach concepts and develop skills when students are so diverse?" Let me suggest three thoughts for your consideration.

First, the burden of accommodation begins with the professor, not the students. Susan Ellis calls for an integrative approach with a variety of innate and alternative approaches being used by instructors.[21] The

---

20. David Lose, "Teaching Preaching as a Christian Practice," in Thomas G. Long and Leonora Tubbs Tisdale, ed. *Teaching Preaching as a Christian Practice: A New Approach to Homiletical Pedagogy* (Louisville: Westminster John Knox, 2008), 47.

21. Susan S. Ellis, "Models of Teaching: A Solution to the Teaching Style/Learning Style Dilemma," *Educational Leadership* 36:4 (1979): 274–77.

responsibility to adapt is with instructor who must acquire skills so as to be able to teach in responsive ways. While it may be challenging, the burden is theirs and not their students'. To borrow loosely from the apostle Paul's desire to be "all things to all people," professors must be flexible so content can be accessed—and ultimately students can achieve greater competency in their preaching.

Fortunately, professors should not find this accommodation as challenging as they might think. As Kenneth Henson and Paul Borthwick write: "There is certainly no shortage of avenues through which educators can match teacher styles with learner styles."[22] During my many years in the classroom, I've found it necessary to acquire new methods. And while a creature of habit, I've found innovation to be refreshingly enjoyable.

Second, students share a level of responsibility and need to get out of their comfort zones. While preferences are well established, students can't always get their way. Certain subjects need to be taught in specific ways. Bill Cerbin's comments are helpful: "If you are thinking of teaching sculpture, I'm not sure that long tracts of verbal descriptions of statues or sculptures would be a particularly effective way for individuals to learn about works of art."[23] Similar words apply to the field of homiletics.

Third, professors should recognize that as responsive as they may attempt to be, they will not be able to satisfy every learner. Awareness, adjustments, and alterations can enhance learning among men and women. Varying methodologies can make a real difference in people's lives. Yet a lingering dissatisfaction is likely to remain and not everyone will benefit. Nevertheless, because of our efforts, more students can be ministered to in unprecedented ways.

CONCLUSION

In preparing men and women to preach, you must remind yourself that your work is not ordinary, but that of a shepherd entrusted with caring for a flock. As shepherds are diligent, doing as much as possible to ensure

---

22. Kenneth T. Henson and Paul Borthwick, "Matching Styles: A Historical Look," *Theory into Practice* 23, no. 1 (1984): 7.

23. William Cerbin, "Understanding Learning Styles: A Conversation with Dr. Bill Cerbin," interview with Nancy Chick (University of Wisconsin Colleges Virtual Teaching and Learning Center, 2011).

their flocks' well-being, you too must respond similarly to your students. Understanding learning styles and responding appropriately can be instrumental in achieving this objective.

Yet your instruction dare not be utilitarian. It is to be from the heart, for eternal matters are at stake. As such, this chapter is not simply an appeal to functionally respond to students' styles, but a heartfelt call to put yourself under the influence of the Holy Spirit in fulfilling your heavenly calling.

5

o o o

What a Freshly Minted Preaching Professor Needs to Know (Part 1)

TONY MERIDA

> *It is a solemn thing to preach the gospel, and therefore*
> *a very solemn thing to attempt instruction or even*
> *suggestion as to the means of preaching well.*[1]

"Can you send me all of your notes from your preaching class?"

"How do you structure your preaching class?"

"What should I be thinking about when teaching a preaching class?"

These are questions other preaching professors have recently asked me. One is nearing the end of his PhD and has been asked to teach as an adjunct. Another professor normally teaches in another discipline but is preparing for a course on preaching to meet a particular need at his institution. The other friend is a retired pastor—now a newly appointed professor of preaching—who wants to give the last chapter of his life to training ministers.

Freshly minted preaching professors look different, but most have the same basic desires. They want to be faithful and effective instructors. They realize the importance of preaching. They love the church. Often, novice preaching professors have plenty of experience in preaching, but they realize that teaching preaching is a different task. Many find teaching preaching much more difficult than preaching.

My retired pastor friend, Nelson, recently visited me in my office. He's a man I greatly admire. He has been a faithful Bible expositor for years on the West Coast. I was humbled that this saintly man would ask a relatively

---

1. John A. Broadus, *A Treatise on the Preparation and Delivery of Sermons* (New York: A. C. Armstrong, 1890), xv.

young professor for help. I told him that I was writing a chapter on what a new preaching professor needs to know. He quickly took out his notebook and pen and said, "Tell me everything; I need help!" Unfortunately, I had to tell him that I hadn't written the whole chapter yet. But our discussion did help me, as I worked through my syllabus with him and as I tried to answer his questions.

After dialoging with my friend and other aspiring preaching professors, I decided to collect the talking points from those interactions. I then sent out an email to the preaching faculty at Southeastern Baptist Theological Seminary to add their thoughts to my notes. Finally, I added some notes from our previous meeting at Gordon-Conwell Seminary, which revolved around teaching preaching. What follows is a collection of these thoughts. While I don't assume to know everything about teaching preaching, and while I'm still learning myself, I do think the following list would have served me well when I started teaching homiletics over ten years ago.

Many tend to mimic preaching professors without considering their own gifts and interests, the changing dynamics of the classroom, the uniqueness of this generation of students, and the broader changes in the pastorate and church. Before shaping your approach, think about these matters carefully. Hopefully the following set of challenges will help new preaching professors prepare for the task: (1) know your goal; (2) know homiletics; (3) know the subjects related to preaching; (4) know your students; (5) know the heart; (6) know the pulpit; (7) know the classroom; and (8) know the needs of the church.

KNOW YOUR GOAL

Preaching professors train students primarily for the local church, not the academy or the conference circuit. The goal isn't to simply transfer information about homiletics. It is to train an army of faithful and effective biblical preachers.

In an age of rock-star speakers, many students crave the spotlight. I often say, "We need a million Bible-preaching, people-loving, Christ-exalting pastors, not twenty more sensational conference speakers who say that same thing at different events." This vision is why I teach preaching. I want to help train and deploy an army of preachers who will say "thus says the Lord" to the ends of the earth.

In John Stott's classic book *Between Two Worlds*, the saintly minister stated, "The essential secret [to effective preaching] is not mastering certain techniques but being mastered by certain convictions."[2] If this is true, as I believe that it is, the preaching professor's job involves helping students form particular convictions about preaching, not merely giving public speaking tips. These convictions will not only help them be effective but also help keep them faithful in the preaching ministry throughout a lifetime.

The question "What makes a faithful and effective preacher?" will help formulate courses on preaching. Granted, you can't do everything in every course. Some courses may be more preparation oriented, some more historically driven, and others more delivery focused. Nevertheless, this overarching question can help inform each type of class. Below is what I would tell students to pursue if they want to grow as effective Bible preachers:

1. Love for the word of Christ and the Christ of the word

2. Love for people

3. Spiritual gifts

4. Homiletical instruction

5. Preaching experience

6. A mentor

7. Preaching models

8. Personal holiness and a vibrant prayer life

9. An understanding of the sovereign Spirit of God

From these nine qualities, they should next consider their particular class and find ways to emphasize these components to some extent.

Students must be taught to love the *word of Christ and the Christ of the word*. They need to preach out of an overflow of a love for the Savior, who is the hero of the Bible. They must be exhorted to live in the word. The

---

2. John Stott, *Between Two Worlds: The Art of Preaching in the Twentieth Century* (Grand Rapids: Eerdmans, 1982), 92.

word should lead them to the pulpit, rather than the pulpit forcing them into the word.

Likewise, with a *love for people*, students need to remember that they aren't just firing an information machine gun from the pulpit. Rather, they're communicating to people—people *they* have been called to love and people that *Jesus* loves.

Regarding *spiritual gifts*, students need to know that God disperses his gifts sovereignly. Not everyone has strong preaching gifts. Students need to live in light of this reality. They need to find their role in the body of Christ and be happy in it. They need to see that they're accountable for what God has given them, not for what God has given to others. They need to accept that preaching involves both divine gifting and skill development—and they should focus on the skill development aspect.

Skill development falls under *homiletical instruction*, which preaching teachers provide in every course on preaching. Some skill development will be more preparation focused or delivery focused. But students must be told to take both preparation and delivery seriously. Many students are good at exegesis, but poor at communication. Others are good communicators, but their content isn't worth communicating! Both types of students need homiletical instruction.

Students also need *preaching experience*. In some classes, teachers of preaching can provide practical experience, but they should also emphasize the need to preach outside of class in various contexts. I tell students to preach at nursing homes, prisons, or any church function that requires public proclamation. I also encourage them to work through a passage of Scripture in a one-on-one setting with kids or students in their local church.

Further, *a mentor* is a great blessing and help to students. Many of the nuts and bolts of pastoral ministry and preaching are learned in life-on-life relationships. There's no blueprint for how one can learn from a mentor. Mentoring may involve structured or informal meetings. It may involve one student and a pastor (or preaching professor), or it may involve a handful of students learning from one leader. Whatever the case, students should be encouraged to learn from godly leaders in mentoring relationships.

Similarly, preaching teachers should encourage students to study various *preaching models*. Good preachers listen to good preachers, so preaching professors should point them to good examples.

Because the preacher's life is tied to the pulpit, they must also empha-size *personal holiness and prayer*. How these disciplines are fleshed out in each class will vary, but the emphasis should be present in each meeting.

Finally, preaching professors should encourage students to marvel *at the sovereign Spirit of God*. There's ample mystery in preaching, including how and why God uses certain preachers. Students should learn to marvel at how God uses the "foolishness of preaching" to save sinners. The wind blows where it wills, and students should remember that preaching isn't formulaic; it's dynamic.

Know then what makes a faithful and effective preacher. Your list may look different from mine. But know your goal and build your courses with this end in mind.

KNOW HOMILETICS

Obviously, a preaching professor should know the basic elements of homi-letics. These basics include, but aren't limited to: a theology and philosophy of preaching, preparing and delivering biblical messages, the relationship between hermeneutics and homiletics, the nature of the pastorate, the history of preaching, models for preaching, and the relationship between prayer/godliness and preaching. A practical basic element involves teach-ing students to discern the main theme of a text and how to make a big deal about this theme in the sermon.

Various books are written on these fundamental subjects, and the preaching professor should be able to produce his own work in written form as well. Every new preaching professor should aspire to write on some aspect of preaching. Writing will improve the professor's teaching, capture his thought for the coming generation, impart his theory more deeply, and contribute to the broader field of preaching.

Exceptional preaching professors not only teach these fundamentals but also engage recent developments and challenges for preachers. There are seven recent developments evangelical preaching professors must think about and address biblically, philosophically, and practically.

CHRIST-CENTERED PREACHING

I can't speak for all evangelical seminaries, but where I teach, this sub-ject greatly interests students. Many students have a great interest in the redemptive-historical nature of Scripture. They want to know how to integrate biblical theology with expository preaching. Professors should therefore be able to not only articulate a philosophy of Christ-centered preaching but also point students in the direction of good resources for further study.

While this renewed interest in Christocentric hermeneutics and homiletics is exciting to me, there are some real dangers preaching teachers must teach students to avoid. These dangers include allegory, flattening the Bible, making questionable and fanciful connections to Christ, and leaving the selected text too soon. I tell students to expound the historical particularities of the text and point out the theological themes in the text. Many older expositional philosophies failed to instruct students regarding the latter. They failed to teach students how to make inner-biblical connections that point to Christ. They failed to teach students how to show where a theme began and where it culminated. So I'm glad students want to avoid "Christless preaching," but it's critical preaching teachers guide them in how to do Christ-centered preaching responsibly.

PREACHING AND CULTURAL ENGAGEMENT

Each generation presents unique challenges to preachers. It's important that preaching professors understand these challenges so they can teach students how to apply the biblical text. In other words, the preaching professor needs to teach students about faithful contextualization. They need to teach students how to establish a point of contact with their hearers so that they may then establish how the gospel connects with them—that is, to sympathize with the skeptic lovingly, to acknowledge their arguments respectfully, and to contend for the gospel skillfully.

Professors must help students think about how to address the unbeliever. Students need to think about whom they quote in sermons and how they sound to the unbeliever. As my seminary president Danny Akin says, "What we say is more important than how we say it, but how we say it has never been more important." Instructors must teach students to use accessible and freshly explained vocabulary. Common theological terms should be used, but these terms must be explained clearly and even memorably. Students also need to learn how to talk about opposing viewpoints accurately and respectfully. It takes a long time for many people to believe, and preachers should want unbelievers to keep coming back. Unbelieving friends will be driven away by inaccurate representations, lack of character, poor argumentation, or a cheap shot taken from the stage at their particular tribe.

MULTI-SITE PREACHING

Like it or not, today's student's world is the world of multi-site churches. Students want to know what the preaching professor believes about this movement—not simply what the professor believes about multi-site *churches*, but also their view of multi-site *preaching*. And the preaching professor needs to be prepared to give an answer to their questions.

THE "LAYMAN'S SEMINARY MODEL" OF PREACHING

Various preaching approaches exist in evangelical churches today, but one popular approach is for the pastor to teach in a professor-like manner for fifty minutes to an hour. When I first went to seminary, I rarely heard anyone preach this long. But today, it's not uncommon, especially in young church plants, to have longer sermons filled with robust theology.

Stylistically, the popular preachers of the older generation were often more oratorical, poetic, and emotional. While many of these preachers continue to bear fruit, students' heroes today tend to speak in a more conversational and didactic manner. Often their heroes speak with a flat screen TV beside them, going from one slide to the next to make points.

Aspiring preachers should think about this trend. Is this movement positive or negative? Why or why not? What should be remembered and avoided if they adopt this professorial approach? Preaching teachers need to talk about this trend in class.

THE SHARED PULPIT

Another trend among younger evangelical pastors and churches is to have a team of preachers. I know of a large church in Texas, filled with younger believers, that uses a team of competent preachers. The founding pastor only preaches about 60 percent of the time. Preaching professors need to talk about the strengths and weaknesses of this approach, and if one chooses this model, how to do it well.

SERMON-BASED SMALL GROUPS

Many students are in churches that don't have Sunday school, but also don't use any weekly curriculum. In fact, the church where I pastor doesn't use any curriculum for small groups. We will occasionally read a book together as a group, and we make lots of books available to people in our book nook, but our week-by-week small group ministry involves trying to apply the text from the sermon. This streamlined approach keeps the whole church on the same page, and it also affects how the preacher approaches application in the sermon. The preacher can say, "Here's a good question for your groups this week." In this way, the sermon isn't the only place where people are engaging the selected text. This impacts sermon preparation, and preaching professors should think about this growing trend as they teach preachers about how to do application and how to lead the church from the pulpit.

PREACHING AND CHURCH PLANTING

In my world, there's a growing trend of students pursuing church planting. Often the best students want to plant new churches instead of pastor legacy churches. This is a wonderful movement, but the preaching professor needs to understand something about church planting to best equip these students.

I have pastored in both contexts, and they are distinct. While the commitment to exegesis is the same, the rhythm of the week is much different. Application differs. Church plants tend to be in urban environments. They also tend to reach younger people and have more unbelievers present in the worship gatherings. All of this calls for extra thoughtfulness in crafting a sermon.

KNOW THE SUBJECTS RELATED TO PREACHING

If you're going to teach preaching, you need to know not only the subject of homiletics but also the disciplines associated with homiletics. One of the reasons I enjoy teaching preaching is because it involves so many disciplines of study: theology, hermeneutics, Bible survey, sociology, apologetics, ecclesiology, missiology, spiritual formation, skill development, and more. Homiletics professors do more than tell students, "Don't talk with your hands in your pockets!" There's more to this job than some of the common stereotypes preaching professors convey. Preaching professors actually need to be able to teach (at some level) various disciplines.

STUDY WIDELY

Ideally, preaching professors will read widely. But unfortunately, most only have time to read sermon preparation material and resources in their major field. They don't have time to read a great number of books outside these areas. So then, it's important to think about how to study theological trends in other ways. I have found that by attending theological societies, and by reading scholarly journals, I stay current with recent theological trends. From this high-level look I can then study particular issues more deeply.

INTERACT WITH OTHER PROFESSORS

One of the gifts of teaching in an academy is the benefit of spending time with other professors. Preaching professors should intentionally mingle with professors of theology, history, biblical studies, and so on to learn personally, and also to better prepare to teach today's students. A few years ago, some colleagues started a "no agenda lunch" in which we would bring our own lunch and simply interact once a week. I find these types of meetings to be not only encouraging but also enlightening. I always learn from my colleagues when we spend time together. I often leave with ideas for how to improve my class after talking to them about subjects related to preaching.

KNOW YOUR STUDENTS

This need isn't new. Good professors in general know their students' names and needs. Of course, it's harder to know your students in larger classrooms, but you need to try. Use name tags, or put name cards at the desk to try to learn names. Get to know your students' desires, interests, and fears. Plan your class breaks with the hope of interacting with different students each week. Put a different name on your calendar each day and pray for that student on that day. Have them in your office and in your home if possible. Don't just "deliver and exit." That's the UPS man, not an excellent professor! The best professors take a real interest in their students. They mentor them, not merely instruct them.

When you know your students, you can also make adjustments to your class schedule. You should have some blend of form and flexibility in your lesson plans. Make adjustments based on the types of students in class. Some classes may have a lot of aspiring international missionaries. You may want to think about how to incorporate lessons on Bible storying or cross-cultural communication. Some classes might have a great number of relatively new believers. This should impact some of your teaching methodologies. Some classes may have students preaching in more urban poor environments, or others in more upper class suburban environments. These needs should be addressed. The point is, you don't merely teach, you teach *students*.

Knowing your students also helps you slow down or speed up in your lesson plans. After talking to some students after my lectures, I have found that they really didn't understand everything. Imagine that! If that's the case, it's critical to make adjustments and revisit material. Know your students, and constantly evaluate and tweak your schedule and your material.

One way you might revisit the material without falling too far behind in your schedule is by recording some videos. These can be viewed by students on their commute or at home at their convenience. Today, time with students doesn't need to be limited strictly to the classroom. It's okay to say via video, "Hey, after talking with some of you, I want to revisit the issue of preaching from wisdom literature. We need to move on to preaching from the prophets, but I want to address three areas of possible confusion surrounding what I said about wisdom literature."

If you know the knowledge level of your students, you can know what to explain further, regardless of what method of explanation you use. But the point is to know what they're thinking. Consider having mini-meetings with students. Or have them turn to a friend and explain what you just said. Tell them to write a five-minute summary on a note card after your lecture and hand it in so that you can see what they know. Give a quick, oral pop quiz, saying, "Johnny, explain to me what expository preaching is and isn't." Find ways to know what your students know.

KNOW THE HEART

Knowing what students know is not the end of the matter. Pay attention to the heart—your heart and your students' hearts.

Preaching professors (and all seminary professors for that matter) need to teach and model prayer alongside the ministry of the word. They need to stress the importance of maintaining a vibrant walk with God.

KNOW YOUR HEART

It's important to guard your own heart as a professor. You will encounter many temptations. Spiritual warfare is real for the professor, not just the pastor! You will be tempted to get angry with students when they seem disinterested, or when they fail to do good work. You will encounter periods of discouragement. You will be tempted to find your identity in your accomplishments rather than in your union with Christ. You will be tempted to compete with other professors. You will be tempted to be puffed up by your writing, speaking, and popularity. Unhealthy ambitions may cause you to grow discontent. Prolonged periods of study may keep you from appreciating the beauty of creation and experiencing biblical community with others.

So then, pursue godliness. Don't mistake great theological knowledge for spiritual maturity. Teach out of the overflow of a heart captivated by the Savior. Practice the means of grace. As George Mueller used to say, get your soul happy in the Lord each morning.

KNOW YOUR STUDENTS' HEARTS

When students ask for recommended books before entering seminary, I usually have Paul Tripp's *Dangerous Calling* at the top of my list. Tripp points out many of the common heart problems related to pastoral ministry. But this book isn't just for students. I think every seminary professor should read it too. Tripp writes out of both professorial and pastoral experience.

Tripp exhorts readers to make the classroom more *pastoral*. Here's a word to all professors:

> I am convinced that the crisis of pastoral culture often begins in the seminary class. It begins with a distant, impersonal information-based handling of the Word of God. It begins with pastors who, in their seminary years, became quite comfortable with holding God's Word distant from their own hearts. It begins with classrooms that are academic without being pastoral. It begins with brains becoming

more important than hearts. It begins with test scores being more important than character.[3]

Tripp goes on to critique theological education:

> If you would go back, let's say, a hundred years, every professor in the classroom would be a churchman. He would have come to theological education by means of the pastorate. In these men there burned a love for the local church. They came to the classroom carrying the humility and wisdom gained only by their years in the trenches. They taught with the hearts and lives of real people in view. … They came to the classroom knowing that the biggest battles of pastoral ministry were fought on the turf of their own hearts. They were pastors who were called not to quit pastoring but to bring pastoral love and zeal into the eco-system of theological education.
>
> But over the years theological education began to change. … Academized Christianity, which is not constantly connected to the heart and puts its hope in knowledge and skill, can actually make students dangerous. It arms them with powerful knowledge and skills that can make the students think they are more mature and godly than they actually are.[4]

Bring a pastoral heart to the classroom. Learn to shepherd students. Address particular sins like self-righteousness, lack of gratitude for the gospel, impatience, lust, greed, the wrong perspective on ministry, lack of real communion with Christ, and other heart problems.

This emphasis also means addressing the preaching *motives* of students, which can be hiding in "subtexts" in sermons. Subtexts are the messages underneath one's message. When a person's heart is not in the right place, the subtext may be, "Aren't I great?" or "Isn't our church great?" Aim to fill students' affections with Christ, so that the subtext of every sermon is "Isn't Christ great?"[5]

---

3. Paul David Tripp, *Dangerous Calling: Confronting the Unique Challenges of Pastoral Ministry* (Wheaton, IL: Crossway, 2012), 52.

4. Tripp, *Dangerous Calling*, 53–54.

5. See Tim Keller, *Preaching: Communicating Faith in an Age of Skepticism* (New York: Viking, 2015), 200–205.

If a student's ability surpasses his or her maturity and love for Christ's glory, then he or she is a walking disaster zone. Unfortunately, I can rattle off a list of names of students (and professors) who are no longer pursuing ministry, or are no longer in ministry because they failed to tend to their own heart. Strive to be a professor who is concerned about heart application as much as theological information.

Students also need to be taught to make all of their theological studies and the preaching professor's class an act of spiritual devotion. In an address to theological students, B. B. Warfield emphasized the importance of maintaining a vibrant walk with God while studying:

> It is possible to study—even to study theology—in an entirely secular spirit. ... Whatever you may have done in the past, for the future make all your theological studies "religious [spiritual] exercises." ... Put your heart into your studies; do not merely occupy your mind with them, but put your heart into them. They bring you daily and hourly into the very presence of God; his ways, his dealing with men, the infinite majesty of his Being form their very subject-matter. Put the shoes from off your feet in this holy presence![6]

Pray that your classes will have a sense of divine glory to them and that students will want to "take notes on their knees" as they consider the God who has called them to preach.

KNOW THE PULPIT

To teach preaching, the preaching professor "should preach often and preach well."[7] Preaching professors need to set an example for students. Students should learn by sitting under their professor's preaching, not just from the professor's lecturing.

Preaching professors teach best when they teach with fresh examples of preaching experiences in mind. When students ask particular questions, having an answer that's related to a recent week's sermon can be helpful, lively, and impactful.

---

6. B. B. Warfield, *The Religious Life of Theological Students* (reprint; Phillipsburg, NJ: P&R, 1992), 5–6.

7. A statement from personal correspondence with my mentor and fellow preaching professor Jim Shaddix.

If possible, the preaching professor should also take students along when preaching at various events. The discussion before and after the preaching event can be insightful and memorable.

Further, because preaching professors want to inspire students, not just inform students, they should exemplify a sincere love for the work of preaching. You will do well to remember the sagely advice from William Perkins's classic work *The Calling of the Ministry*. The old Puritan lamented the "scarcity of true ministers" saying that "good ministers are one in a thousand."[8] To help stir up more for effective pastoral work, he said: "Let each minister both in his teaching and his conversation work in such a way that he honors his calling, so *that he may attract others to share his love for it*."[9] Every preaching professor should ask, "Is my present ministry of the word attracting students to share in a love for preaching the word?"

Preaching professors should also be preaching regularly to authentically express a belief in the power of preaching. It's difficult to convince students of the potency of the pulpit if preaching teacher aren't preaching themselves. Instead, the preaching professor should express Martyn Lloyd-Jones's view, both verbally and by example. He said, "What is it that always heralds the dawn of a Reformation or of a Revival? It is renewed preaching. Not only a new interest in preaching but a new kind of preaching."[10] Preaching professors should teach and live as if they believe this, and may their students burn with fire in their bones to herald God's gospel.

KNOW THE CLASSROOM

One of the biggest challenges for freshly minted preaching professors is transitioning from the pulpit to the classroom. In the pulpit, you know your approach. It doesn't change much. It's usually a monologue and typically follows a week of preparation and internalization of the biblical text. But in the classroom, good professors provide occasions for dialogue and other in-class activities. This shift is perhaps more challenging for preaching

---

8. William Perkins, *The Art of Prophesying with The Calling of the Ministry* (reprint; Carlisle, PA: The Banner of Truth Trust, 2002), 96.

9. Perkins, *Art of Prophesying*, 96 (italics mine).

10. D. Martyn Lloyd Jones, *Preaching and Preachers*, 40th anniversary ed. (Grand Rapids: Zondervan, 2011), 31.

professors than other professors because they are so accustomed to passionate monologues.

Therefore, aspiring professors need to adjust their expectations for each class period. Not every class needs to be a monologue. Sometimes your class should involve discussion, debate, and dialogue. You can stir up a passion for preaching using these approaches, in addition to your fiery monologues.

When I first started teaching, I thought mainly about lecturing. While I'm still a supporter of the lecture, and do a great deal of it, I have had to learn the discipline of planning and facilitating helpful dialogues and other forms of education. I have had to integrate learning techniques such as sermon viewing/evaluation, small group book discussions, and personal journal reflections on assigned Bible texts into my classes.

Aspiring preaching professors should constantly evaluate the class and consider using some different methods of teaching. I have benefited greatly by asking other professors what kinds of instructional exercises they are using.

KNOW THE NEEDS OF THE CHURCH

Because the preaching professor is training students for the church, not the classroom, he needs to be aware of some of the current issues in the church today. Let me mention a few of the issues students need to think about as they prepare for the ministry of the word.

PROMOTING CHRIST-CENTERED HOLINESS IN A SEX-CRAZED, SEX-CONFUSED WORLD

Pastors today counsel people with countless sexual problems. Just when I think I have heard all the twisted ways one could sin with pornography, I hear yet another wild case. It's almost weekly. Regularly, I am talking with someone who has questions regarding sexual orientation. "Why can't I be gay and be a Christian?" is just one of many commonly asked questions. Adultery is an ongoing problem. Singles also need answers.

Thus, you must strive to help your students prepare for this world—a world with which they're familiar. Help them think about how to apply Scripture to all forms of sexual matters. Encourage them to aim to change worldviews, not just behavior. Teach them to preach the whole narrative of

Scripture and avoid proof texting. Help them learn to make these hot topics theological, not political. Teach them to love broken people—mingled with an unwavering boldness and willingness to be ridiculed for preaching the Bible. Remind them that they aren't looking to win popularity contests but to honor the God who called them.

PROMOTING CHRIST-CENTERED ETHNIC DIVERSITY IN A DIVIDED WORLD

Students should also think about why and how they will preach on gospel and race within the context of the storyline of the Bible (creation, fall, redemption, new creation). They should seek ethnic diversity for the sanctification of the church and the church's witness to the world for the glory of Jesus—who is no tribal deity but the Lord of the nations. For the person preaching the Bible, the opportunities to deal with this emotionally charged subject are presented throughout Scripture. When coming across passages that call for application on Christ-centered unity, preachers must learn to speak winsomely, wisely, compassionately, and boldly. They must have an unwavering confidence that Jesus can overcome darkness and break down walls. As they preach in a compelling way, they should also work and pray for a teachable spirit among the listeners.

CULTIVATING REAL COMMUNITY IN A SOCIAL MEDIA WORLD

The younger generation knows they need community, but many aren't willing to make the sacrifices necessary to make it happen. Social media provides unfulfilling community. Today's students need to learn both the value of biblical community and how to apply the text to the community, not just individuals. They must keep in mind that Christianity is personal, but it's not individualistic. People are starving for biblical community, and the preacher must help lead others into community by teaching it, modeling it, and providing an on-ramp to experience it. Preaching professors should help students think about how to preach for the good of community formation.

INTEGRATING FAITH AND WORK IN A COMPARTMENTALIZED WORLD

Another failure in many sermons today is the failure to apply the text to people's vocations. Often application involves three main exhortations:

"Pray more. Evangelize more. Give more." While emphasizing these disciplines is important, the sermon and the workplace should intersect frequently.

Excellent preaching professors will help students learn how to apply the text to one's vocation. Many in the church don't see the relationship between faith and work. They live in a sensationalized world, and they need to know how "ordinary Christians" can make an extraordinary impact in the day-to-day rhythm of life.

DOING EFFECTIVE EVANGELISM IN A SKEPTICAL WORLD

Preaching professors need to help students think about the relationship between evangelism and the weekly sermon. This involves both mobilization and evangelistic application. Regarding the former, it's important to help students think about how to encourage people to do the work of evangelism. Older forms of evangelism involved crusade evangelism, street preaching, and door-to-door evangelism. While not discounting the value of these methods, one method that appears to have both historical precedent and present fruitfulness is network evangelism. In his book *Cities of God*, professor Rodney Stark documents how Christianity spread through social networks. It grew as people shared the gospel with family members, friends, and coworkers. If the preacher adopts this type of evangelistic approach, then he should drip this evangelistic application into each sermon.

Regarding evangelistic preaching, preaching professors need to help students think about how to address unbelievers from the pulpit. I encourage my students to address the unbeliever in the introduction and to have some apologetic sidebars planned within the body of the sermon.[11] Finally, they should address the skeptic in the conclusion and invite people to respond in faith or to respond with a follow-up meeting in which they can ask questions.

Students will improve in evangelistic exposition by simply being involved regularly with unbelievers. If they live isolated lives, then their sermon application will reflect this lifestyle. Students should also consider addressing their "old self" in the sermon and avoid preparing sermons for

---

11. I'm greatly indebted to Tim Keller's thoughts on preaching to skeptics.

their peers. They should think about the common questions they used to raise, their former interest level, and their former capacity to understand sermons to make their sermon accessible and impactful to the skeptic.

Preaching professors will develop their own convictions related to evangelism in today's world. Whatever these convictions are, strive to integrate them in your preaching classes.

CONCLUSION

One of my homiletical heroes is John Broadus, the late preaching professor at The Southern Baptist Theological Seminary. In 1865, Southern had only a handful of students. And Broadus had only one student in his preaching class—a blind student, Mr. Lunn. Because this student couldn't benefit from a written text on homiletics, Broadus developed detailed notes on preaching. Broadus wrote to his wife saying, "Really, it is right dull to deliver my most elaborate lectures in homiletics to one man, and that a blind man."[12] Here's the wonder of the story. People still benefit from his lectures to Mr. Lunn. From theses lectures, Broadus laid the foundation for one of the most influential books ever written on preaching, still in use today (though revised), titled *On the Preparation and Delivery of Sermons.*[13]

What did Broadus know? He knew that his work mattered, and that he ultimately worked for the glory of God. Regardless of how many students you have, give yourself to it wholeheartedly. Every freshly minted preaching professor needs to know that they work to the glory of their great God, who saved them through Christ Jesus, and empowers them for the work of training and deploying an army of gospel-centered preachers.

---

12. Cited in Thomas J. Nettles, *James Petigru Boyce: A Southern Baptist Statesman* (Phillipsburg, NJ: P&R, 2009), 219.

13. Ibid.

6

o o o

What a Freshly Minted Preaching Professor Needs to Know (Part 2)

BLAKE NEWSOM

It is a solemn thing to preach the gospel, and therefore
a very solemn thing to attempt instruction or even
suggestion as to the means of preaching well.[1]

What do an accomplished executive chef and champion mixed martial arts fighter have in common? They have mastered the art of integration—blending various skills and disciplines into a productive whole for the purpose of accomplishing a unique goal. An accomplished chef is more than a grill master or sandwich artist. She takes various culinary distinctions and fuses them together for a cornucopia of taste. Moreover, the executive chef assumes the responsibility for multiple dimensions of the culinary experience, including kitchen oversight, staff issues, menu creation and selection, and budgeting and purchasing, as well as meal and restaurant aesthetics. For the executive chef, the taste of the meal might be the most important element, but it certainly is not the lone element. Quality is required in each subsequent part as it is in the whole product. Consequently, the executive chef must be adept at integrating multiple dimensions affecting the culinary experience.

For the champion mixed martial arts fighter, the essential nature of integration is embedded in the title. Although he begins in one type of fighting, the "mixed" martial artist naturally extends into other branches of fighting. The mixed martial artist learns to integrate boxing, kickboxing,

---

1. John A. Broadus, *On the Preparation and Delivery of Sermons*, 4th ed., rev. Vernon L. Stanfield (New York: Harper and Row Publishers, 1979), xxv.

judo, wrestling, jiu-jitsu, and a broad range of other fighting disciplines in his quest to become a complete fighter through consolidating diverse combat tactics into a more effective synergistic whole.

As in the case of the accomplished executive chef and the champion mixed martial artist, integration is also necessary in the practice and instruction of homiletics. The effective preaching professor learns to consolidate various disciplines for a fruitful aggregate. In a certain sense, the homiletics professor serves as the tip of the spear of multiple disciplines at theological academic institutions, merging biblical studies, theology, Christian counseling, Christian education, pastoral ministries, and other disciplines to teach students to present truth in a clear and compelling manner.

As I quickly discovered, teaching homiletics can seem overwhelming due to the breadth of the disciplines involved and the weight of the responsibility of such a task. Teaching someone to preach at times can feel like preparing someone to perform on Broadway, realizing the potential for enormous success or epic failure on the part of the student and consequently the professor. However, the preaching professor has more on the line than the performance instructor in that eternity is at stake. Despite the sometimes overwhelming urge to flee (brings to mind an MMA fight) under the mountain of responsibility, the preaching instructor must assume his or her position in front of the class and instruct the students in the highest calling this side of eternity. The following is a humble attempt of an often-overwhelmed preaching professor to help you in the high and holy assignment of preparing messengers of God to proclaim the word of God to the people of God.

PRACTICE WHAT YOU PREACH

SPIRITUAL VITALITY

Preaching is first and foremost spiritual work. Consequently, teaching preaching should be considered spiritual work. Each semester a new crop of students comes into our classes with the intention of developing as communicators of God's word. The Holy Spirit and spirituality in general are too often assumed and consequently overlooked in preaching texts and classes. However, Christian preaching and the homiletics classroom must not be devoid of the Spirit or spirituality. The student need not be under the impression that hermeneutics and homiletics alone make the Christian preacher, so the preaching instructor must go to great lengths to remind students of the spiritual nature of the role and task of preaching. Put another way, an atheist theoretically could take classes in biblical studies, theology, hermeneutics, and homiletics, and subsequently have the knowledge base and skill to develop and present a sermon. However, no one would think of the atheist's discourse on the Bible as true Christian preaching. It is essential for preaching instructors to convey the sentiment that true Christian preaching is spiritual, starting in the life of the preacher.

To convey the value and role of spirituality in preaching, the preaching instructor should model spiritual vitality and provide a healthy spiritual environment in the classroom. At some level, it is incumbent upon the teacher of preaching to embody the charge of Lloyd-Jones: "The preacher's first, and the most important task is to prepare himself, not his sermon."[2] With this in mind, homiletics classes need to maintain an emphasis on spiritual vitality. Consequently, preaching instructors should include discussions and lectures on prayer and other spiritual disciplines as well as conversations on worship. Students should leave the preaching class with the experience of having been in a healthy spiritual environment, not one of emotionalism or excess but of true, biblical worship and spiritual vitality.

The instructor sets the tone for this sort of environment to be possible. While there will always be elements of a person's spiritual walk not able to be displayed in the classroom environment, there are elements that most assuredly could be displayed and encouraged to the students. As Paul told the Corinthians to follow him as he followed Christ (1 Cor 11:1), so the preaching instructor should represent spirituality to preaching students, thereby providing a living example of spiritual vitality to the students.

PERSUASIVE TEACHING

Inherent to the field of homiletics is the role of and emphasis on persuasion and ancient rhetoric. Aristotle, whose work provided the foundation, formalization, and proliferation of ancient rhetoric, defined rhetoric as "the faculty of discovering the possible means of persuasion in reference to

---

2. D. Martyn Lloyd-Jones, *Preaching and Preachers* (Grand Rapids: Zondervan, 1971), 166.

any subject whatever."[3] Christian preaching seized upon the benefits and effects of rhetoric by fusing rhetorical principles into the proclamation of the Christian message. Rhetorical practices flourished as rhetoricians such as John Chrysostom and Augustine applied their rhetorical prowess to the communication of Holy Writ, but rhetorical principles also are embedded in Scripture, demonstrated in rhetorical structuring within the Pauline corpus. From the earliest days through contemporary times, rhetoric and Christian preaching have been inextricably connected, which makes obvious sense given the task of the preacher charged with persuading listeners toward following Christ.

Given the role of rhetoric in preaching, the instructor should not only be mindful of but also engaged in the art of persuasion as he or she seeks not only to lodge information into the mind of the student but also thrust passion into the heart and skill into the action of the student. Simply put, teaching implies the impartation of information, inspiration of values, and instruction of behavior. At the core of education is transformative communication, meaning effective communication must occur for education to occur. Augustine noted the three functions of rhetoric: to teach, to delight, and to sway.[4]

Modeling rhetorical skills and practices is vital for the preaching instructor as he or she incorporates the art of persuasion into the pedagogical methodology, being precise in organization and purposeful in content as well as persuasive in delivery. Teaching homiletics must be undertaken with a keen sense of the desired result in the life of the student. Preaching is different than biblical studies or theology. A biblical studies or theology professor teaches to prepare the student for scholarly study and interaction, but the subsequent communication of that body of knowledge by the student is not necessarily emphasized in the studies. However, given the emphasis on communication and persuasion in preaching, the preaching instructor is forced to recognize that the manner in which ideas and information are communicated and transmitted is perhaps as vital in the preaching class as the ideas and information being taught. Students who

---

3. Aristotle, *The Art of Rhetoric*, trans. John Henry Freese (Cambridge: Harvard University Press, 1994), 15.

4. "Augustine: The Uses of Rhetoric," in *The Company of the Preachers: Wisdom on Preaching—Augustine to the Present*, ed. Richard Lischer (Grand Rapids: Eerdmans, 2002), 284.

have observed the art of persuasion demonstrated effectively will be more likely to value and implement it in their own practices.

FINDING YOUR VOICE

The Greek maxim "know thyself" is a helpful reminder for the professor of homiletics since the temptation to either teach as one has been taught or teach contrary to how one has been taught is powerful. The best teacher knows himself, including strengths and weaknesses regarding preaching and the teaching of preaching. In preaching, the sentiment often is conveyed through the expression "finding one's voice." Since preachers tend to start preaching after having heard other preachers, the challenge for the new preacher is to discover one's own approach to the task of preaching. Therefore, discovering one's own homiletical style, or finding one's voice, is a significant part of the growth process. The goal for the preacher is to preach in a manner befitting the uniqueness of the individual rather than counterfeiting another.

The same sentiment is true for the preaching professor, who must find his voice, which is the discovery of the personal style in which he will teach. Discovering a personal approach to the teaching endeavor will serve the preaching professor in an inestimable manner. The legendary and influential homiletics professor John Broadus regarded style as a preacher's "characteristic manner of expressing his thoughts, whether in writing or in speech."[5] Elizabeth Achtemeier boldly expressed, "Style is the man!"[6] The importance of discovering and maintaining a personal flavor cannot be overstated, particularly as related to the field of homiletics. The preaching professor cannot help students discover their voice when he has not discovered his own.

While fidelity to personal style is important, the preaching professor's teaching style should be consistent with the best pedagogical methods. One aspect of pedagogy particularly germane to homiletics is the interplay between the deductive and inductive approach to teaching. This issue is particularly important given the discussion within the field of homiletics

---

5. Broadus, *On the Preparation and Delivery of Sermons*, 200.

6. Elizabeth Achtemeier, *Creative Preaching: Finding the Words* (Nashville: Abindgon, 1980), 92.

concerning best practices regarding deductive and inductive preaching, and these considerations highlight the unique issues for the teacher of preaching. The instructor of homiletics must be aware of personal bias regarding the two divergent approaches and settle on most effective pedagogy rather than personal preference.

Personally, I teach deductive and inductive preaching in my classrooms, and I model deductive and inductive preaching in the pulpit. However, I subordinate style to context and audience. While I preach deductively more frequently, I teach inductively in the classroom more frequently. The point is to be intentional about the most appropriate pedagogical method and to deftly integrate (there's that word again) personal style with best pedagogical practice.

The deductive approach places importance on the learning of principles or concepts that are explained, developed, and applied at a later period. Conversely, the inductive approach depends upon the students engaging in processes and activities while learning the principles or concepts as encountered or needed. For the homiletics course, the deductive approach might have the teacher lecturing through the sermon development process after which the student develops a sermon. However, the inductive approach might have students engaging in the process of studying a text from which they collaboratively develop a sermon with the teacher highlighting important principles throughout the process.

My desire is for students to engage the text as early and often as possible. I want them investigating the text and developing a sermon from the text. Consequently, I use more of an inductive approach, guiding students through the homiletical process while explaining principles. I have found this approach to benefit students as it pertains to sermon preparation and development. With this approach, the sermon development process becomes more real and practical than theoretical.

THEOLOGICAL, PHILOSOPHICAL, AND HISTORICAL FOUNDATIONS OF PREACHING: THE *WHY* BEFORE THE *HOW*

Shifting to the nuts and bolts of teaching preaching, the preaching instructor should begin with the foundational components of preaching: theology, philosophy, and the history of preaching. The theology of preaching addresses the *why* of preaching and provides the foundation, infrastructure, and motivation for preaching. The best theology of preaching is guided by Scripture and consequently focused on answering the question: What is God's perspective concerning preaching? The student needs familiarity and interaction with Scripture's teaching concerning the essential nature and role of preaching so that a firm foundation is laid. If the *why* is solidly understood, the *how* will be more readily appreciated.

The instructor should provide opportunity for students to develop their personal theology of preaching so that their theology is not secondhand and sterile. Instead, it will be direct and active, having been forged from their theological ruminations so their future preaching ministries will be firmly anchored to God's word. Instructors must help students understand how their theology of preaching is affected by, and consequently must address, a host of issues. In developing their personal theology of preaching, students should be encouraged to consider factors including but not limited to the nature and authority of God's word, the role of the Holy Spirit, the nature and purpose of worship, the call and role of the preacher, and the purpose of the preaching event. Since students' theology of preaching will shape and guide their preaching throughout their ministries, the homiletics instructor should ensure that this aspect of preaching receives the instructional time deserved.

A personal philosophy of preaching, which begins to answer the *how* of preaching, flows directly from the person's theology of preaching. While a theology of preaching examines preaching from God's perspective, a philosophy of preaching examines preaching from the preacher's perspective. A philosophy of preaching provides perspectives on issues influencing and influenced by a person's preaching ministry, determining approach to the text, sermon, audience, and a host of other issues pertinent to the preaching ministry and life of the church.

The student of preaching needs a safe environment in which he or she can surmise the impact of a personal theology and philosophy of preaching. The preaching instructor should guide discussions and provide feedback to students concerning these foundational aspects of preaching that will have far-reaching effects in their students' preaching ministries. Many disagreements occupying the field of homiletics fall into the categories of theological and/or philosophical disagreements. While using the classroom as an opportunity to engage the students on the most biblically and culturally appropriate approaches to preaching, the instructor need not shy away from discussing disagreements, while also sharing his or her own theology and philosophy.

In addition to theological and philosophical foundations, the history of preaching should receive instructional treatment in the homiletics course. As in other academic disciplines within Christianity, history is replete with versions of best and worst practices that can prove beneficial in the instructional merit afforded such a topic. Consequently, time allotted in the preaching course to cover the history of preaching will prove substantive. Within a discussion of this topic, one could address the cultural factors affecting the state of preaching as well as approaches to preaching and representative preachers within the major epochs of Christian preaching. In the history of preaching, the student will find the expansive impact of preaching throughout the centuries into all areas of culture and society, including but not limited to geopolitics, customs, morals, science, art, philosophy, literature, and education.[7] The student of preaching will also have the added benefit of his or her personal theology and philosophy of preaching being sharpened by the beliefs and practices of prominent and influential historical figures, while learning from the mistakes of previous generations of Christian proclaimers.

SERMON DEVELOPMENT

After the theological, philosophical, and historical foundations of preaching have been laid, the homiletics instructor can shift the course focus to sermon development. The process of sermon development is the approach by which one arrives at the sermon to be preached.

Ideally, the sermon development process begins with a biblical text, an issue that should be addressed in the theology and philosophy section. The sermon that does not originate with a biblical text has an inherent weakness: it originates from a source that is not authoritative and infallible. Consequently, the preacher is dispensing ideas that seem helpful but lack the authoritative nature and transformative ability of the Bible. Personally, I prioritize expository preaching since this type of preaching originates in

---

7. Edwin Charles Dargan, *A History of Preaching*, vol. 1 (Grand Rapids: Baker, 1954), 8–12.

and develops its content from Scripture. While this type of preaching is not the only type of preaching, expository preaching is the most faithful to the authorial intent of Scripture; therefore, expository preaching should be the bread and butter of preaching ministries. Homiletics instructors would do well to encourage students toward this method of preaching to promote the best environment for spiritual transformation to occur in their students' preaching ministries.

The following step-by-step outline of teaching sermon development focuses on the preparation of an expository message. The recommended instructional plan is not intended to be an exhaustive treatment of the sermon development process but rather to overview basic steps of developing an expository sermon. It is not intended as a homiletics textbook but as an overview of the sermon development process from the standpoint of the instructor, seeking to answer the question: How does the homiletics instructor teach sermon development in a step-by-step process? Familiarity with the field of homiletics, including concepts of preaching as well as basic and helpful resources for sermon development processes, is assumed.

SELECTION OF THE TEXT

Assuming the biblical text provides the content of the sermon, the homiletics instructor must help the students understand the steps of sermon development that are focused on the text: selection of the text, study of the text, and development of the text. Since the best sermons begin and take shape from the biblical text, the instructor of preaching should anchor the students in the biblical text. Students should be encouraged to focus on and devote themselves to the biblical text as the source of content for sermons, beginning with text selection. The various methods of text selection, including systematic exposition of extended portions of Scripture, or a more spontaneous week-to-week approach to text selection, should be discussed and explained to the student with the positives and negatives of each being highlighted.

STUDY AND DEVELOPMENT OF THE TEXT

Next, students need to become familiar with the complex and intricate process of textual study, which includes studying the selected biblical text as well as outside sources. However, before consulting outside works, the students should be encouraged to immerse themselves in the biblical text. Teachers of preaching must doggedly press students into the text before pushing them from the text to outside sources. The student should be challenged to read and reread the text multiple times. The surrounding verses and chapters also are to be read so that the student has an understanding of the general and immediate context of the text as well as the text itself. The great preacher and teacher of preaching Robert Smith Jr. recommends reading the text fifty times in an effort to grasp it. While homiletics teachers might not press students to that level of reading, they do need to be inspired and challenged to devote themselves to reading the text multiple times.

The benefit of multiple readings of the text is found in the student's ability to contribute to the interpretive task regarding the text rather than running blindly to outside sources for interpretation. However, the benefit of outside sources cannot be overlooked as they help interpret the biblical text through the following means: background studies, word studies, grammatical and syntactical studies, and theological studies. Previous study in the field of hermeneutics will prove advantageous for the instructor and student as they delve into textual study. Study tools are growing in availability and accessibility for contemporary preachers, and these tools should be discussed in the classroom setting. The preaching instructor should advise as to best resources and best practices regarding resources. Of particular help to the student will be the instructor's expertise as to wise stewardship regarding purchasing resources. I would recommend that the teacher develop a tiered list of resources for homiletical helps ranging from necessary to beneficial.

Transitioning from the study of the text to the sermon requires the student to analyze the natural structure of the text, which provides the structure of the sermon. I recommend demonstrating a helpful approach to textual structuring, whether it is through a more robust and intricate approach such as grammatical diagramming or through a simpler approach such as textual phrasing.[8] Whatever approach the instructor takes, the

---

8. *Phrasing* is a term used by William D. Mounce. I recommend familiarizing yourself with his approach to phrasing the biblical text. See William D. Mounce, *Greek for the Rest of Us: Essentials of Biblical Greek* (Grand Rapids: Zondervan, 2013): 93–115, 199–213.

student should see the merits of structuring the text in a way that helps transition to the structure of the sermon.

DEVELOPMENT OF THE MAIN IDEA OF THE TEXT AND SERMON

The next stage of sermon development is the discovery of the big idea, or main idea, of the biblical text and sermon. The general exegetical outline of the selected pericope provides a clearer picture of the overall message of the biblical text, and will help the preaching student understand how to determine the big idea. Since the main idea of the sermon flows from the main idea of the selected biblical text, the student will be positioned appropriately for discovering the big idea after studying and outlining the text. The main idea of the text is that on which the text focuses. The main idea of the sermon is that on which the sermon focuses. Since the main idea of the sermon is developed from the main idea of the text, the biblical passage is the driver and catalyst of the sermon. In this stage, students should learn not only to discover the main idea of the text but also to transition the main idea of the text, which is stated in the past tense of the biblical world, to the main idea of the sermon, stated in the present/future tense of the contemporary world. The present/future tense of the sermon main idea is the rifle shot of the sermon around which the sermon is built and through which the sermon has focus and punch.

I recommend spending significant time on this particular area of the development process by enrolling students in big idea discoveries and discussions, working together to decide on the best, most textually accurate main ideas. I have found group work to be particularly helpful in this area. The majority of group work done in my classes is focused on examining and discussing a biblical text followed by determining the main idea of the text and sermon. The students need to engage in this discussion in a controlled group to simulate the sort of inner dialogue of proposition development that will occur in the individual sermon development process throughout their preaching ministries.

DEVELOPMENT OF THE SERMON BODY

After the main idea is established, the spine of the sermon is intact and ready for the remainder of the sermon's muscular-skeletal system, which should derive from the outlined/structured biblical text and gather around the main idea. At this point, students will have done the most difficult work in that they have analyzed and structured the biblical text, which provides the sermon structure. The teacher's role is to help students see the connective points between the text and the sermon as well as the benefit of developing the sermon structure from the biblical text. The main idea of the text drives the main idea of the sermon, which is delineated into the main points of the sermon. All the pieces of the sermon connect with one another and connect back to the text. The main points of the sermon, which support and delineate the main idea of the sermon, are next broken down further and explained by the functional elements: explanation, argumentation, illustration, and application. The preaching instructor must carefully help the students understand the various workings of each step in this process. The teacher is to serve as a guide through the steps of sermon development, ensuring students' understanding of each step so they have the necessary expertise and skill to duplicate this process over the course of their ministry.

FINISHING TOUCHES

The final stage of sermon development is the smoothing of the sermon, which at the completion of this stage should be focused, clear, forceful, and complete. This concluding aspect of sermon development includes determining the introduction, conclusion, title, tone, and other finishing touches. Teaching these aspects of sermon development can, however, prove difficult; the instructor should provide helpful generalized tips without crossing over into personal stylistic preferences. For this stage, the teacher can use other preachers to emphasize the powerful force of introductions, conclusions, titles, and other dimensions of preaching by referencing or even showing examples crafted by skilled preachers. The students will more than likely benefit from seeing polished sermons and ideally will be inspired to a level of excellence in their own preaching.

SERMON DELIVERY

After the sermon has been developed and finalized, the work is far from over since it must be proclaimed. Students often mistakenly assume a sense of completion when the printer is spitting out the sermon or the sermon has been transferred to the mobile device for preaching. However, the sermon is not a message until it is delivered to listeners—the act of sermon delivery—which homiletics teachers must also address with priority. Helping students minimize distractions so that the word is delivered clearly is a tremendously valuable function of a homiletics instructor.

While providing tips about sermon delivery can prove insightful, there is no substitute for giving a student feedback on an actual sermon. The best pedagogical processes allow students to preach and receive feedback during their course work. In providing feedback to the preaching student, I see the homiletics instructor filling two important roles. In one sense, the teacher must convey the sense of evaluation and criticism to prepare the student for the realities of the preaching ministry. Bruce Theilmann states it well: "To preach, to really preach, is to die naked a little at a time and to know each time you do it that you must do it again."[9] Critique is an inevitable and unenviable dimension of preaching that homiletics instructors must communicate when preparing preachers. Although critique on the part of the preaching instructor is not the most enjoyable dimension of teaching, preparing future preachers for a life of critique while also helping them minimize future opportunities for negative criticism due to weaknesses in their preaching is rewarding in the long term.

The primary role of the preaching instructor as it pertains to sermon delivery is to help students realize oral communication problems of a general nature and deficiencies specific to the individual preacher. To borrow from Jeffrey Arthurs's four-step process for gaining awareness and improving skill in oral delivery,[10] the homiletics instructor's role is to help students move from unconscious incompetence to unconscious competence. This process of improvement begins as the student becomes aware of distracting mannerisms, moving from unconscious incompetence to conscious incompetence. After becoming aware of distractions, the student can progress to conscious competence, the stage in which improvement occurs. Finally, the student hopefully improves to the point of unconscious competence, the stage at which the distracting mannerism is gone without the student's persistent concentration on removing the distraction.

---

9. Bruce W. Thielemann, *The Wittenburg Door*, no. 36 (April–May 1977).

10. Jeffrey D. Arthurs, *Devote Yourself to the Public Reading of Scripture: The Transforming Power of the Well-Spoken Word* (Grand Rapids: Kregel, 2012), 71–73. I encourage a thorough reading of Arthurs's work for improving oral delivery.

The preaching instructor should help students through this difficult process, pointing out their distractions while also pointing out their strengths. There is no safer environment for this to occur than the homiletics classroom. Instructors are to encourage students in their calling and assist them in becoming clear, precise, and articulate communicators so that the word—not the preacher's distractions—holds the audience's attention.

CULTURAL DIAGNOSTICS

While the nature and role of the audience is always looming over the sermon development process, the audience naturally gains attention in the stage of sermon delivery. There is no message without an audience, a fact of which students need reminding. Preaching is not an attempt to transfer words on a page; preaching is an attempt to deliver a message, which implies a sender and receiver. As Haddon Robinson states, "We don't teach the Bible. We teach people the Bible."[11] Preaching instructors should help students see the need for understanding the communicative process. Often, I see preachers withdrawn into the pulpit bubble attempting simply to say what is on the pages in front of them rather than proclaiming a prepared and personalized message to listeners. Instructors should help students disengage from the pulpit bubble so that they might engage the audience with a relevant message.

I consider preachers to be cultural diagnosticians. They are to investigate, analyze, and diagnose the state of culture so they can determine the most culturally appropriate manner of delivering the cure with biblical fidelity. This entails knowing the audience and the cultural influences shaping the audience. Again, Robinson offers this advice: "The most important single factor in whether or not you are an effective communicator lies in whether or not you doggedly pursue [the question] 'Who are my listeners?' "[12] With this in mind, homiletics instructors should recognize their role in helping preachers become better diagnosticians. Preaching is not done in a vacuum but in a particular context to a particular people.

---

11. Haddon W. Robinson, foreword to *Preaching to a Postmodern World* by Graham Johnston (Grand Rapids: Baker, 2001), 7.

12. Robinson, foreword to Johnston, *Preaching*, 7.

The better the preacher knows the audience, the more likely the message will be received.

I take my students through four questions to stimulate their thoughts about culture: Who are we? Where are we? When are we? Why are we? The questions are intended to discover and discuss the nature of people in the current time period in this culture and the reasons people are the way they are. Ideally, the questions serve to diagnose prevailing worldviews and to engage issues, including matters of theology, ethics and morality, politics, and other societal factors in the church and secular culture. The goal of this discussion is to ignite a passion for the people to whom preaching students will minister as well as incite them to be cultural diagnosticians.

If homiletics instructors can kindle an excitement for cultural analysis while simultaneously guiding students through initial diagnostics, students will be better communicators of the timeless message within a given context. Teachers should also encourage students to adjust their individual style to a particular setting of culture. Broadus stated over a century ago but with prescient insight:

> Style must have regard for the times. As Christianity moved out into the gentile world, the style of preaching changed. It followed the customs and tastes of different peoples and different ages ... but its excellence has been its ability to sense the intellectual and emotional dispositions and tastes of a given age and relate itself to them effectively. Whenever preaching has failed to do this and become merely imitative of another age or some prophetic hero ... it has lost in power. And history's road is strewn with the bones of ineffective imitators.[13]

Preaching instructors should not desire simply to duplicate themselves but should hope to produce culturally relevant ministers who know the times and can communicate effectively in the culture to which they are sent.

MAINTAIN RELEVANCE

Maintaining relevance is not only important for the preacher but also for the preaching instructor. Homiletics professors need to stay up-to-date

---

13. Broadus, *On the Preparation and Delivery of Sermons*, 204.

with preaching and teaching trends. Knowing cultural shifts affecting preaching as well as how successful preachers are relating to people is vital. Reading academic journals as well as practical periodicals will help in acquiring a sense of cultural and preaching trends. I also recommend sampling from other sources, such as podcasts and the Internet, which have made maintaining relevance much easier than in previous times. Simply perusing the top one hundred podcast preachers provides a plentiful sample of a wide range of preachers from various backgrounds, denominations, and styles. Personally, I try to regularly sample popular preachers, even those with whom I disagree theologically and methodologically, since their popularity means that they are communicating their message with some appeal. Knowing how popular preachers are gaining listeners and large audiences is an important component of being a cultural diagnostician—and this requires listening to what popular preachers are saying and how they are saying it. Sampling broadly provides an understanding of trends in culture and preaching.

Finally, to improve effectiveness as a teacher, strive to increase technological relevance. Regis Philbin famously avoided the Internet and technology, saying they were a passing trend. While his behavior and speech were intended to be funny, there are instructors who simply by avoiding technology are missing opportunities to be more proficient. Beneficial technological tools abound and can be leveraged by homiletics instructors to equip preachers more thoroughly. Homiletics teachers should be the most cutting-edge instructors in the theological institution (perhaps outside of youth ministry professors), since they are the ones who are immersed in and engaging culture most consistently.

CONCLUSION

Remembering the sober charge of James 3:1, homiletics instructors have a monumental task from God. As you fulfill your calling to equip ministers, remember to follow God, love your students, work hard, and be teachable. Each year I continue to tweak lectures, presentations, activities, and curricula after realizing a better approach. Honestly, I hope this remains true as long as I teach because that means I will be working to continually improve at the task to which God has called me. The fact that you are reading this book is proof of your desire to improve. Be encouraged.

The accomplished executive chef might have begun as a dishwasher and the champion mixed martial artist might have started taking beatings in a dingy gym, but their tireless efforts and continued growth eventually resulted in reward. Do your best to grow and improve each year, and God will reward you and your students.

7
o o o

Developing a Syllabus for a Homiletics Course

SID BUZZELL

The best educators thought of teaching as anything they might do to help and encourage students to learn. [1]

A syllabus matters.[2] It may be seen as a distracting interruption to the important task of course preparation, but it matters. Organizing the nuts and bolts of schedules, assignments, and grades isn't nearly as interesting as delving into the books and articles that supply material for class lectures. But a few hours invested in writing a "good" syllabus will streamline the preparation process and produce a far better course.

This chapter addresses two questions about writing a syllabus. First, what is the purpose of a course syllabus? Second, how can teachers write a good syllabus that serves that purpose?

WHY WRITE A SYLLABUS? WHAT'S ITS PURPOSE?

A good syllabus focuses on what students should learn in the course, what the teacher and the students will do to pursue that learning, and how students will demonstrate their success in learning what the course

---

1. Ken Bain, *What the Best College Teachers Do* (Cambridge, MA: Harvard University Press, 2004), 49.

2. You may be tempted to read this chapter about writing a syllabus first because you have to write a syllabus. But do yourself, your school's administration, and most importantly, your students the favor of reading chapters 1–6 of this book before you start writing your syllabus. Chapters 7 and 8 depend heavily on the previous six chapters. The mechanics of writing a syllabus and defining instructional outcomes are essential parts of effective teaching. But you will be far more effective in accomplishing both of those tasks if you have an informed understanding of how learning and teaching work.

was designed to help them learn. A good syllabus serves three purposes: it contributes to students' learning, it helps teachers create and teach the course, and it helps the administration.

A GOOD SYLLABUS CONTRIBUTES TO STUDENTS' LEARNING

Because most students want to be successful, knowing what success looks like and how to achieve it is important to them. A well-written course syllabus tells students three essential things. It tells them what they should be striving to achieve by clearly identifying and stating the course goals. Second, it outlines a path to those goals by providing a clearly designed course schedule that tells students what they will be expected to do in their pursuit of those goals. And third, it explains how they will demonstrate what they have learned and how those demonstrations will be assessed and graded. In short, a good syllabus tells students what they will learn, how they will learn it, and how they will demonstrate their success in learning it.

The whole process of course design begins with defining what the course intends to help students learn. A course with clearly stated learning goals gives students a rationale for each assignment and class session. Students know that their work in the course is carefully designed to produce a result they understand and value. Course activities, assignments, and exams are justified because they relate to course goals. When students understand how their work contributes to their learning, they are more intrinsically motivated.

A syllabus also creates a road map through the course. When preaching professors provide a clear schedule that states what each class should accomplish, students understand what their teacher hopes to accomplish in each session. Each assignment can then be linked to a class session with a clearly stated goal. Students know what they should be doing and why. A syllabus that unambiguously describes what students should do on each assignment removes guesswork and allows them to focus on what the assignment was designed to help them learn. Explaining these facts in a syllabus minimizes ambiguity, confusion, and guesswork. It allows students to focus on what the assignment was designed to contribute to their learning.

After explaining what the course is designed to help students achieve and what they should do to achieve it, the syllabus should explain how their learning will be assessed and their grades earned. At this point it is important to explain that teachers do not assign grades to students. Teachers report on how students performed on each course assessment. Students earn grades and teachers communicate what grade a student earned on each assignment, quiz, exam, or presentation—and other criteria the syllabus identifies that will contribute to student assessment. When teachers provide a clear grading scale and consistent feedback on assessments throughout the course, students can monitor their success. They can see early warnings of a poor course grade and adjust their performance or be encouraged by their good work as the course progresses.

The syllabus also contributes to students' success in a course by explaining a few important personal facts. First it is important that preaching instructors briefly present their educational values and philosophy. This helps students understand what they can and cannot expect from their professor, and what their professor will and will not expect from them. Students will understand why they are given certain assignments and why class sessions are conducted as they are. They will understand how the professor grades their work. When a clear philosophy, values, and expectations are expressed to students, preaching professors contribute to a more relational environment and invite students to see their teachers as fellow learners.

A GOOD SYLLABUS HELPS TEACHERS NAVIGATE THEIR WAY THROUGH THE COURSE

A syllabus helps a teacher in at least three important ways. First, writing the syllabus forces the teacher to make important decisions about the course's design. Second, a syllabus guides the teacher through the course and helps keep them focused and on track. And third, a good syllabus minimizes the angst, ambiguity, and sometimes anger associated with grades.

Thinking clearly about course goals, procedures, and assessment while writing a syllabus helps design a course that is streamlined and coordinated. The thought and time invested in writing a syllabus can save a great deal of confusion and frustration for both students and teachers. Selecting each course component thoughtfully and intentionally because it contributes to accomplishing a specific learning goal allows the teacher to confidently and enthusiastically present that component as an essential part of the course.

When each textbook, online resource, and in-class experience is selected because it contributes to students' learning something specific, each activity makes more sense to the student. When course activities are designed to focus on goals, teachers can prepare and conduct class sessions with greater intentionality and focus. If students ask why they have to complete an assignment or participate in a class activity, the teacher can explain the rationale for it. In fact, it is helpful to explain that rationale to students even if they don't ask about it. Knowing how an assignment or activity contributes to student success makes it more motivating. The thoughtful process of writing a syllabus forces the teacher to make these important decisions about what to include and exclude from each course.

A syllabus provides a road map for both students and teachers because it guides both along the same clearly stated path to the same clearly stated destination. Assignments can be synchronized with class sessions to prepare students for more active participation. The teacher's preparation is focused because he has stated clearly what each session is designed to accomplish. He is never left guessing what to do in the next class session because he has made those decisions ahead of time. Each session is intentionally and intelligently sequenced and designed to contribute to the larger course purpose.

A section in the syllabus that explains assignments and grades is an essential component of any syllabus. Writing this section of a syllabus forces the teacher to think clearly about how students earn grades. A clear explanation of what each assignment, quiz, and exam contributes to their overall grade will help students see grading as more objective and fair. Teachers can more fairly and confidently put a grade on an assignment when the grade is based on stated criteria. If a TA grades the paper, he or she does so using the same standard the student was expected to use when writing the paper. When a student's work doesn't earn the grade they want, the teacher can confidently and fairly explain the grade based on its description in the syllabus. Clearly stated learning goals will help teachers design assignments, quizzes, and exams that make sense to students because they are each linked to a specific learning goal. Teachers can grade them objectively, and when students receive their grades on their work, they are more apt to see the grades as fair and just.

A well-written syllabus establishes an informal contract with students that minimizes the guesswork and subjectivity that can lead to confusion, frustration, and angry disputes. Teachers do themselves and their students a huge favor by investing time in a well-written syllabus.

A GOOD SYLLABUS HELPS THE ADMINISTRATION

A well-written syllabus is important to the school's administration for two main reasons. First, course syllabi provide information administrators need to evaluate courses, instructors, and exams.

Second, a syllabus also documents what was taught in a course, what the faculty member's credentials are, what grade level the course qualifies for, and how many credits it grants. When other schools request information for transfer students or when an accreditation team visits, syllabi are essential documents. If they are well written they serve the administration well.

PREPARING TO WRITE A SYLLABUS

Before writing any important document, including a syllabus, you need to gather some essential information. That information comes from a number of institutional sources and is readily available.

An important first step is to check with the department chair or dean to see if the school has a standardized syllabus format. Many schools provide a template with essential information already included. That saves some writing (and possible rewriting) time and assures that the syllabus conforms to the school's standards.

You should also ask if your class is one in a multiple-section course. If it is, the syllabus will have to mirror the other sections in that course. There may be some room for independent design, but much of the syllabus information should match what is in the other sections of the same course. Accrediting agencies want sections of a course to be—to a large extent—the same.

To write a helpful syllabus, you need answers to some questions about the students who will be in the course. You need to know what courses students have to complete before taking this course and what those prerequisite courses covered. Otherwise there will be gaps or overlap in your course. You must know if you can cap enrollment, and if not, how many students will be in the course. The answers to these questions will influence the course schedule and classroom activities.

You also need to know if this is a required or an elective course. Required courses often include students who need additional motivational information in the syllabus.

Because each course you teach makes a specific contribution to a larger curriculum, it is essential that you identify where the course is placed in the curriculum. If you are writing a syllabus for Homiletics 1, you should check the syllabus for Homiletics 2 to identify what that course requires students to know when they begin. If the syllabus is for a Homiletics 2 course, you should check the Homiletics 1 syllabus to identify what students have already studied. If the course has been taught previously, gather earlier syllabi to generate ideas for your own syllabus.

It is also helpful to ask about the course's reputation at the school. Ask how previous students who took the course felt about it. Ask to see previous course evaluations if possible. Students talk to one another about such things, and it helps to know where you are starting and if you need to subtly explain in the syllabus that there are some different approaches to the course this time around.

Before writing a syllabus, check out the classroom where the sessions will meet. This will influence what you can actually do during the course. Is it a regular classroom, a preaching lab, or some other space? Does it have fixed or movable seating? Does the room have tables or desks? Is it possible to rearrange the room or exchange the furniture if needed? What equipment is available? Is there a whiteboard, smart board, document reader, media projector, classroom computer (Mac or PC), etc.? Will there be a camera available to record student presentations? Before designing the kind of learning experiences you want to include in the course, it is important to find out what is and isn't possible.

Then identify what day and what time of day the class is scheduled. Identify any all-school events that will take students out of class and factor them into the course schedule. Count exactly how many total class days are available. Ask administrators if exams are required or optional for this course. If the course has multiple sections, find out if quizzes and exams have to be the same for all sections or if each teacher has flexibility and how much.

As you prepare your syllabus, it is essential to think through exactly what students must know and do to succeed in the course so you can focus on the essentials and eliminate the nonessentials. Then, clearly state those essentials as the course goals and identify what you plan to do in the course to help students achieve those goals.[3]

Once goals are defined, begin to identify what you will do in the course to help students achieve each goal and identify the specific point in the course where each goal will be addressed. Some goals are best addressed in class and some through homework assignments. Some goals are more complex and are complicated enough to require multiple exposures. It is important to make those decisions before you write your syllabus.

Next, design homework assignments and make certain that each one is justified by its relationship to a specific learning goal. Decide which assignments are designed to prepare students for class participation and which are designed to provide feedback on how well they can perform on what they have learned. Check to make sure assignments are appropriately weighted so more and less complex assignments earn an appropriate number of points toward the students' final course grade.

You also will want to identify other resources that are available to add dimension to your course where appropriate. Find out which other faculty members could speak to certain topics—or parts of certain topics. Ask if there are local experts who could address specific topics. If you invite an outside resource, ask if the school can pay a stipend to visiting lecturers, and how much. Find out if visiting lecturers need to be and if so, by whom. Identify online tools that will help students achieve specific goals.

At this point you can determine how you will assess student achievement—and describe that in your syllabus. Decide which goals you can measure best with quizzes and/or exam questions and which ones are best measured by a paper or project. Identify what feedback process best allows students to demonstrate competence on each goal. Justify all assignments, as well as quiz and exam questions, by identifying how they provide students opportunity to demonstrate a specific competency. Irrelevant and/or "make-work" assignments distract students from learning and diminish their incentive to participate in the course. Check to see that

---

3. For more on how to do this, see chapter 8, "Learning Levels and Instructional Intentions."

any forms used to evaluate student performance match course goals and indicate which are the most important. For instance, telling students what to include in a sermon introduction but not evaluating those things when they preach is counterproductive.

Once you have answered these questions, and before writing your syllabus, design and/or read your end-of-course and mid-course evaluations. Ask yourself what questions students will be responding to on the school's end-of-course evaluation and whether your course design reflects these institutional values. Also, be sure to prepare an early student evaluation form that allows students to express likes and dislikes around the middle of the semester. End-of-course evaluations can frustrate students because it's too late to change anything.

WRITING YOUR SYLLABUS

At this point you have a preliminary understanding of what you want students to know and do and what you will do to help them succeed. The final step is putting this information together in a single document so you and your students can agree up front on the "who," "what," "how," "when," and "why" of each aspect of your course. You can write this document, called a syllabus, in such a way that if a student—or an administrator—asks at any moment during the course, "Why are we doing this?" you can open your syllabus and explain, justify, and if need be, defend it.

As you write your syllabus, make sure it does each of the five essential elements a good syllabus must do, as described below.

A GOOD SYLLABUS SETS A TONE FOR THE COURSE

The syllabus is usually the first thing students see in a course and tells them how the course contributes to them as a person and as an effective practitioner. Your syllabus should help create a climate of eagerness and anticipation for each part of the course.

It sets a tone, first, by telling your own story. Explain why you want to teach this course and why you are excited about homiletics. List your credentials, which tell students why they should trust you to lead them through this course. You should also briefly describe your teaching/learning philosophy and explain your approach to office hours: Do you prefer drop-ins or appointments? Do you like to "hang out" with students or prefer a more formal style?

Second, it explains what you define as your responsibilities for students' success and what you define as theirs.

A GOOD SYLLABUS INCLUDES THE COURSE'S NUTS AND BOLTS

A syllabus plays an important role by giving students detailed information that they will need to know through the semester. It should list major topics and give a rationale for each. It should clearly state all the course goals. It must be comprehensive so that each goal stated in the syllabus is addressed at some place in the course. When you design your syllabus, eliminate all unnecessary activity from the course and justify everything you ask students to do.

You should also provide a detailed class schedule with dates, assignments, and topics for each session so students can easily identify what they need to do for each class. Schedule and list quizzes, exams, and other variables so students aren't confused or surprised. Make sure there is enough time for all students to do an oral presentation. To paraphrase the familiar saying, "Plan the work so the students can work the plan."

And it is important that you provide a bibliography of required textbook(s) and articles and additional reading.

A GOOD SYLLABUS TELLS STUDENTS HOW TO SUCCEED IN THE COURSE

Students like to succeed. In the academic world, grades are an important indicator of how successful they have been in a course. This means it is important to explain in the syllabus what success looks like and how to achieve it.

Provide as many specifics as possible. State the suggested amounts of time required to complete each major assignment. Clearly describe any group assignments so students aren't confused when they try to participate. State specific criteria for completing a complex and/or complicated assignment so students know what to do to earn the grade they want.

It helps to include any models or illustrations of those complicated assignments. This is especially helpful if a student protests a grade and you need an explanation of that assignment that is clear enough to resolve the disagreement. With a clear grading scale that includes the number of points students will earn for each grade level on each major assignment, they—and you—can track their progress. Check to make sure assignments are fairly weighted so that more complex and time-consuming assignments gain an appropriate number of points in relation to simpler assignments.

A GOOD SYLLABUS SPELLS OUT THE INSTRUCTOR'S EXPECTATIONS

It is important that you clearly describe your absence policy and make certain that it conforms to the institution's policy (if any). State the number of excused absences and the consequences when students exceed the maximum. Include a clear policy on arriving late for class.

Write a clear policy on late assignments and on redoing assignments for lesser or the same credit. Decide and state if you offer extra-credit assignments. Students with lower grades in a course may want to do additional work at the end of the semester. If you don't state an extra credit policy, you may end up creating extra work for yourself instead.

Explain your expected workload for the course. A rule of thumb for undergraduate courses is two hours outside of class for every hour in class. Graduate work is closer to three hours per hour in class. You may want to alert students to the places in the course where heavy workloads will hit them and caution them accordingly.

A GOOD SYLLABUS EXPLAINS SCHOOL POLICIES

Check with your department chair or dean for policy statements on academic integrity, academic freedom, disabilities, and diversity. These policies address legal and ethical issues and should be included in the syllabus to protect the school from illegal procedures and lawsuits. Most schools require each course syllabus to state them. But personal attitudes toward additional sensitivity and effort involved with helping some students succeed are important as well.

Whether you intend it or not, many students and administrators will judge the quality of your course by the quality of your syllabus. This syllabus is most always the first thing they use to evaluate you and your course.

ENCOURAGE STUDENTS TO READ
AND USE YOUR SYLLABUS

The best syllabus ever written helps no one if no one reads it. You can make your syllabus serve your students and yourself by doing a few simple things: print it, hand it out, and discuss it in your first class session. You make a powerful statement about how important the details listed in the syllabus are when you process it in class with your students. Doing so provides time to hear students' questions, fears, disagreements, and other confusions or concerns. In addition, it shows you are willing to adjust things that are problematic by adding or eliminating as necessary. Some things can't be added or eliminated, and you will more confidently hold the line on those if you have carefully thought through and can justify why it is or isn't there. As much as possible, let students help you create the course that will be most effective for them and you. Make any adjustments, reprint the syllabus, and hand it out again. Then you can post it online. Most schools now use services like Moodle or Blackboard, so that is a simple step.

During the course, use the syllabus to answer procedural questions that surface. Treat the syllabus like the agreement it was designed to be. Get students used to using it to answer their own questions. Treat it as an informal contract with your students. Some teachers even include a page that students sign to indicate that they have read, understand, and agree with the syllabus' content. The teacher collects and files the signed agreements in case there is a dispute over grades or other matters. Some also give a graded quiz on the syllabus during the second day of class. The point is to make a clear statement that the syllabus matters—to the teacher and to the students.

SAMPLE SYLLABUS FORMAT

The syllabus format can vary from school to school and department to department. Some allow or even encourage faculty to use cartoons, quips, and artwork to personalize their syllabi. Others treat syllabi more like a formal contract and discourage creative expression. The following template is presented only as a guideline.

INTRODUCTORY MATERIAL

A syllabus' introduction should include: the institution's name; the course title; the semester and year the course is offered; the meeting time and location; the instructor's name, office location, email, and office phone (cell phone optional); and office hours.

EXPLANATION OF THE COURSE

This section motivates students to take the course seriously. It should communicate clearly what the class contributes to students as persons, how it contributes to their academic program, how it contributes to their professional effectiveness, and why you believe this course is important and why you want to teach it.

INTRODUCTION TO THE INSTRUCTOR

Include your professional and educational credentials, your educational philosophy and biases, and relevant personal information: family, interests, hobbies, your dog's name, etc.

COURSE PROCEDURES AND EXPECTATIONS

This section includes the class-session format and expectations for student participation.

It is also important to describe attendance and late policy, late work, reduction of grades, redoing assignments, extra credit, etc. Provide a brief description of group work, presentations, final sermon format, and evaluation forms. It is also helpful to include a statement about courtesy expected in groups, class sessions, and discussions.

INSTRUCTOR'S BIASES AND ASSUMPTIONS

Give students a brief description of your own teaching style. Tell them what they can and cannot expect from you and what you do and do not expect from them. This section should also include office-hours procedures as well as available hours. Briefly describe how you define your role: Are you an instructor, teacher, mentor, or counselor?

COURSE OUTCOMES

Carefully analyze what students have to know and do to successfully perform the tasks required to prepare and preach an effective sermon. Start with broad behaviors and break them down into subordinate behaviors required to "do" the broader behavior. Then break those subordinate behaviors down into even more specific behaviors. See chapter 8, "Learning Levels and Instructional Intentions."

COURSE SCHEDULE, REQUIREMENTS, AND GRADING

After creating learning goals, integrate them with the daily course schedule and with the assignments that will prepare students to achieve the goals for each session. Some assignments will help prepare students for class participation and some will provide feedback on how well they achieved the learning goals. Design quizzes, exams, and other feedback mechanisms that will best measure student achievement. At this point in designing a syllabus, attempt to ensure all possible assignments, class activities, and feedback activities selected are the ones that will best prepare students to achieve course goals and assess how well they succeeded in doing so.

If well written, this section of the syllabus will be referred to in just about every class session to check on how well students achieved the goals and what is required to succeed in the next session. The good syllabus will link all assignments to course goals, link all class activities to course goals, and link all feedback mechanisms to course goals. Chapter 8 will discuss learning goals and objectives. It is important to read that chapter before writing a syllabus.

Because this section relating goals, schedule, and assignments is the heart of the syllabus, I have illustrated below how learning goals, class sessions, and assignments are related in a syllabus. Communicate these relationships so students can clearly see how the work you assign contributes to a specific learning goal. The integrated schedule provides a rationale for each session in your course because students understand which learning goal(s) they are working on and how you have helped them prepare to work on those goals by completing the appropriate assignment.

For instance, in the section of a course where you are helping students discover and write a sermon's big idea, you may state the goal for this section of the course this way:

Goal: Identify the main idea in a biblical text

When analyzing that goal, you may identify the following knowledge and skills a student will need to achieve the goal and generate the following objectives:

Objectives: By the end of this unit each student should be able to:

1. Define and explain the meaning of "idea" as we use it in the course.

2. Explain how we form ideas.

3. Describe and apply the process of identifying a writer's idea(s) in a literary passage.

4. State that passage's idea as an exegetical and as a homiletical idea.

Your next task is to determine what kinds of experiences you can create for students that will help them achieve those objectives, and list them as assignments for students to complete. The following chart demonstrates how you would present the section of your course on identifying the main idea in a biblical text in your syllabus:

Unit Goal: Identify the Main Idea in a Biblical Text

Date	Topic	Preparation for Class Session	Write for Group Discussion
1/17	The preacher and the text's idea 1 (Objective 1)	Fee/Stuart, pp. 11–54. Read your preaching text and one of the suggested commentaries.	One-page summary of what your passage is saying. See model on syllabus, p. 13.

1/22	The preacher and the text's idea 2: What is an idea? (Objective 1)	Fee/Stuart on your genre: Ephesians & Hebrews (55–88) Psalms (205–248) Luke (127–162) Judges (89–125)	One page on how genre influences the exegesis and hermeneutics of your passage. See model on syllabus, p. 16.
1/24	How people form ideas (Objective 2)	1. Robinson, 33–50	Begin exegesis on your preaching passage. See explanation on syllabus, pp. 17–18.
		2. Course notes on ideas, 21–25	
		3. Fee and Stuart, 55–162. Reread Fee/Stuart sections already read.	
		4. Robinson, 51–66	
1/29	How people discover ideas in others' writings (Objective 3)	Complete Step 1 of exegesis: "Studying the Passage Itself." See syllabus, p. 16.	Bring Step 1 of your exegetical paper to class. See model on syllabus, p. 14.
1/31	The idea in YOUR passage (Objective 3)	Fee and Stuart, 163–264 Robinson, 66–70	Complete the steps of stating your idea. See syllabus, p. 9.
2/5	Exegetical and homiletical ideas (Objective 4)	Complete Step 2 of your exegetical paper. See syllabus, p. 19.	Bring your Step 2 work to class.

Assignments, class preparation, and group work are all tied to the objectives. Students know how their reading and written work contributes to achieving each objective. Students experience accomplishment and success throughout the course.

Students receive grades on written work throughout the course so they can track their progress. For the section of the schedule above, I have listed the assignments and the points they contribute toward their final grade (below). This process requires additional thought as you prepare the syllabus, but may save time at the end of the course if students question or challenge their grades.

Week	Date	Assignments	Points	You
1	1/17	Read Fee/Stuart, 11–54.	10	
		Read your passage and one commentary.	10	
		Write a one-page summary of your passage.	5	
2	1/22	Read Fee/Stuart on your genre.	10	
		Write one page on genre influence.	10	
	1/24	Read Robinson, 33–50.	10	
		Course notes on ideas, 21–25.	10	
		Read Fee/Stuart, 55–162.	15	
		Read Robinson, 51–66 ("stop at Stage 3...").	10	
3	1/29	Complete Step 1, "Studying the Passage Itself," of your exegetical paper. See syllabus, p. 16.	20	
		Bring your Step 1 work to class.	0	
	1/31	Read Fee/Stuart, 163–264.	15	
		Read Robinson, 66–70.	10	
		Complete the steps of stating your big idea and bring it to class. See syllabus, p. 9.	10	
4	2/5	Complete Step 2 of your exegetical paper. See syllabus, p. 16.	20	
		Bring your Step 2 work to class.	0	
		Etc.		
		Etc.		

Grade Scale	Possible 675	675–607 = A	606–540 = B	539–505 = C	504–475 = D	<475 = F

You can "contract" for a grade by earning the number of points you need for each grade. Track your progress carefully. Assignments will be returned within two class sessions after you turn them in. Note: I do not "give" grades. I record the points you generate on each assignment and the grade you earned. You are free to discuss why you earned the number of points you received on any assignment within one week of receiving that assignment back from me.

INSTITUTIONAL POLICIES

Ask your department chair or dean for copies of these documents and include them in your syllabus:

1. Academic Integrity

2. Accommodations for Students with Disabilities

3. Inclusivity Statement. This statement assures all students that they are welcome to participate fully in the course. In a homiletics course, some female students or students from a "different" tradition or denomination may need that additional assurance.

CONCLUSION

A syllabus matters. A well-written syllabus includes more than a class schedule and reading assignments. It takes thought and time to write, but when you carefully design and write a good syllabus, you do a great service to the students, the administration, and yourself.

8

○ ○ ○

Learning Levels and Instructional Intentions

SID BUZZELL

> *Instruction is successful, or effective, to the degree that*
> *it accomplishes what it sets out to accomplish.*[1]

At some point in preparing a course teachers have to make the difficult decision about what exactly to include and exclude from a course. They have to decide what to teach and how to teach it. And that's what this chapter is about.

But this chapter isn't so much a chapter about teaching, because ultimately, teaching isn't about teaching. Teaching is about learning. Learning is the end; teaching is the means to that end. Students' learning has to be the driving force of the whole enterprise. No intelligent decision can be made about what to do as teachers until intelligent decisions have been made about what the student should do as a result of their learning from what is taught. Thus, this chapter is about the *process* teachers use to decide what students must learn, how well they must learn it, and how they will demonstrate they have learned it. It is about how to state those three things clearly so both teacher and student agree on what the course intends for the student to accomplish.

Since students' learning is the goal of teaching, it's important to discuss what learning is and how teaching contributes to it. What the *teacher* wants to do, likes to do, or is comfortable doing should not be the focus, but rather how the teacher decides what students must learn *to do*.

---

1. Robert Mager, *Preparing Instructional Objectives* (Atlanta: Center for Effective Performance, 1997), 1.

For instance, if a teacher prepares a first-year course in homiletics, students will have to learn different things than if it's a second-year course or an elective. So regardless of what course is being taught, teachers must begin at the same place. Teachers must identify and clearly state what students must *learn* to successfully *do* what the course promises to teach.

Since teaching is about learning, I will first explore what learning is. Then, since teaching is about preparing experiences that will contribute to student learning, I will discuss how to select those experiences and how to state them so that students clearly understand what they are.

WHAT IS LEARNING?

There are many definitions of learning because people learn different things in different ways. In this chapter, I will use a general definition that reduces learning to its basic elements: Learning is *change in an organism resulting from meaningful interaction with its environment.*

FOUR KEY CONCEPTS IN THE DEFINITION OF LEARNING

First, learning should produce a *change* in the learner. After learning something, students expect to be different than before they learned it. The change may be in their knowledge, their skill, and/or their attitude. The teacher's task is to participate in some way—either directly or indirectly—in that change.

Second, learning is change *resulting from* an experience intentionally designed by a teacher to stimulate change. Change is a fact of life. People get taller and older. Their hair and nails grow. But those changes aren't attributed to any learning experience. To say someone has learned something, change must be connected to an activity that contributed to that change.

Third, any activity teachers use to stimulate change is fruitless unless there is *meaningful interaction* with that activity. These words suggest that the learners are consciously engaged with the stimuli used to contribute to the learning. Students make conscious, informed, and intentional choices to change.

Finally, learning and the teaching that attempts to stimulate it always occur in an *environment*. In a formal learning environment, there are numerous stimuli—some that contribute to learning and some that distract. Some are intentional and some unintentional; some are productive and some counterproductive. One of a teacher's responsibilities is to help students learn by selecting experiences that contribute to what the course syllabus states the course is designed to help them learn and eliminating as many distractions as possible.

SIX LEARNING LEVELS

Teachers want their students to learn but aren't always clear about what they mean by the word *learn*. Anyone who has passed a course in physical science can claim they have "learned" physics. But few would say they have learned physics at the same level as Stephen Hawking. To say students only need to "sort of learn" *this*, but they need to "really learn" *that* doesn't help teachers teach or help students learn either "this" or "that" in any clear sense of the term. To add more precision to the idea that a student should "sort of learn" or "really learn" something, teachers should set learning levels to help clarify that ambiguity.

A learning level is the degree of intensity or sophistication with which one is able to deal with newly acquired knowledge. Learning levels can help teachers clarify what it means that Homiletics 1 students don't learn to preach at the same level they will learn to preach at in Homiletics 2. Learning levels help explain the difference between a "good" final sermon preached in Homiletics 1 and a "good" final sermon preached in Homiletics 2.

It is essential that teachers state the difference between what will be accepted as a good sermon introduction or outline in a beginning homiletics course and what will be accepted as good in an advanced course. Teachers must define how well students need to learn what they are teaching. They must decide what course topics students will have to learn at a high level and what topics they need—at this stage of their development—only be acquainted with. Wrestling with these decisions means wrestling with learning levels.

Benjamin Bloom has broken learning into six levels of sophistication. In the following table, you can see Bloom's learning levels in the left column, followed by activities and outcomes in the center and right columns.

Bloom's learning level	Activity: demonstrate the ability to ...	Illustration of the learning outcome: the student can ...
Remembering	memorize and retrieve previously learned material	1. name the book, chapter, and verse where the Great Commission is stated. 2. recite the Great Commission from memory.
Understanding	grasp the meaning of material	1. describe what a "disciple" is. 2. explain the meaning of "to observe."
Applying	use material in new and concrete situations	1. prepare a five-minute oral explanation of how to become a disciple. 2. describe (in a three-page paper) how being a disciple influences their daily life.
Analyzing	break material down into component parts and explain its organizational structure.	1. explain the difference between "disciple," "baptize," and "teach" and how those words combine to define Jesus' intention in the Great Commission. 2. create a grammatical analysis of Matthew 28:16–20.
Evaluating	judge the value of material for a given purpose and explain judgments citing specific criteria.	1. identify at least one error in a recorded explanation of the Great Commission. 2. name two strengths in a recorded explanation of the Great Commission. 3. explain both 1 and 2 using course material to justify his decisions. 4. prioritize three commentary explanations of Matthew 28:16–20 from most to least accurate, and explain their choices.

Bloom's learning level	Activity: demonstrate the ability to ...	Illustration of the learning outcome: the student can ...
Creating	relate parts to form a new whole.	1. outline an article he would write explaining what Jesus' Great Commission is. 2. prepare a ten-minute presentation explaining to a high school class how to live as a modern-day disciple of Jesus.

THREE REASONS WHY WE USE LEARNING LEVELS

First, learning levels force teachers to define how thoroughly a student must "know" something. It also allows the teacher to construct assignments, class sessions, and feedback devices (quiz and exam questions, papers, projects, presentations, etc.) that are appropriate to the learning level for that knowledge or skill.

Second, learning levels give students a clear understanding of what they must do and how well they must do it to demonstrate that they have "learned" something at the appropriate level. When informing students about how thoroughly they must learn things, direct their attention to the most important parts of the course. Some things will only need to be introduced in a course, and others are essential to student success in the body of knowledge and skills the course is designed to help them master. Applying learning levels to various parts of the course helps students know where to focus. It also helps the teacher to major on the major things and minor on the minor things when designing the course. Some of the minor things are more fun to teach, and teachers may be drawn toward those aspects of the course.

Third, to ethically assign a grade to an assignment, the teacher and the students must have some clearly specified standard that measures levels of success. Both teacher and students can justify the difference between an A and a D grade on an assignment.

Learning is what education is all about. There is a strong temptation for beginning professors to focus on what they want to teach, but that is never the place to begin designing a course. Always begin with *what the student needs to learn* and *how well they need to learn it*. Only then can teachers intelligently decide what and how to teach.

STATING CLEAR INSTRUCTIONAL OUTCOMES

With this brief introduction to learning and its levels, I now want to explore how to communicate as clearly, precisely, and unambiguously as possible what a teacher wants students to learn in a course. This process demands some disciplined work, but what it produces is essential when designing a course, when teaching the course, and when giving students their course grades.

People use different terminology to describe their learning intentions, so for the sake of clarity, I will use the following four terms to describe what should happen when teaching preaching.

I will use the term *result* to describe what students should learn in the whole course. In a beginning homiletics course the result might be stated, "At the end of this course students will be able to prepare and preach an effective sermon." But teachers and students need to know more about what the course is designed to teach than what that general statement says.

There are specific things students need to learn before they can achieve that stated result. For instance, before they can prepare and preach an effective sermon they might have to select and exegete a text well enough to preach it. Then they might have to craft that text into a sermon. And they have to know how to present the sermon they have crafted. Each of those more specific behaviors make up the course result as *outcomes*. These outcomes usually become the units in a course.

Although outcomes inform students they have to "exegete a passage" and "craft and present a sermon," these statements are still too broad. In the same way teachers analyze results, they should also analyze outcomes. When analyzing each of those three outcomes, the teacher should identify some specific things students must learn to achieve each outcome. These more specific things are termed *goals*. Goals often become the theme for one or more class sessions within course units.

The teacher should analyze each goal and generate even more specific things students must learn to achieve each goal. We refer to the specific things students must learn to achieve our goals as *objectives*. Objectives define what teachers are doing in each class.

There is nothing magical or mystical about this process. It is just the hard work of figuring out exactly what students must learn in order to identify as exactly as possible what the teacher must teach.

It is essential to start with the largest overarching behavior students need to learn (results). Then, generate more specific learning statements (outcomes) by asking what people do to perform the broader behavior stated in the result. Analyze those second-level learning statements (outcomes) to identify even more precise learning intentions called *goals*. Finally, analyze these goals and identify what students need to do to achieve each goal; these final and most precise statements are called *instructional objectives*.

For example, in a homiletics course, a broad result could be for students to preach effective biblical sermons. Analyze the behavior required to preach an effective sermon, and identify three outcomes a student must achieve if she is going to preach one effectively:

1. She has to prepare the biblical text she wants to preach.

2. She has to craft that text into an effective sermon.

3. She has to present that biblical sermon in a clear and persuasive manner.

Then, analyze these outcomes to generate their essential goals, and analyze goals to generate their essential objectives.

A diagram of what we have produced with this exercise would look something like this:

Result	**Preach an Effective Biblical Sermon**											
Out-comes	Exegete the Text					Prepare the Sermon						Preach the Sermon
Goals	Exegesis			Text's Idea/ Outline			Intro		Body		Con-clusion	Accu-rate	Clear
Objec-tives	1	2	3	1	2	3	1	2	1	2	1	2	Etc.	Etc.

So, since it is essential

- for the teacher to identify specific intentions of instruction,

- for the student to understand what those intentions are, and

- for both the teacher and students to value each intention enough to pursue it,

then it is essential for the teacher

- to identify those specific intentions, and

- to state them in an unambiguous manner.

Many remember courses where they weren't clear about what they were supposed to learn and, at times, it appeared the teacher didn't either. Until teachers have defined and communicated what success looks like in their course, they can't be successful teachers—and students can't be successful learners.

If you have never read about or attempted to analyze learning outcomes before, it can be confusing. So the following material may require a couple of readings. You will notice that each of the outcomes, goals, and objectives below describes what *you the reader/learner will be doing* after you have successfully read this chapter. As you will discover later, teachers always state these intended results of learning in terms of what *the learner* will do to demonstrate their learning.

It is essential to distinguish between what the teacher will do to assist the learner and what the learner will do to demonstrate how well he has learned. The term "methods" will be used to describe what teachers do. The terms "results," "outcomes," "goals," and "objectives" will be used to describe what students will do to demonstrate learning. Teachers can never make intelligent decisions about teaching methods until they have clearly described what those methods are designed to produce.

The intended *outcome* of this section of the chapter is that by the time you have finished studying the chapter you can define and state instructional intentions that help you teach in a way that students actually learn what you intend, at the level you intended.

To achieve that *outcome,* I aim to help you (the reader/learner) achieve the four *goals* listed below. For you to achieve each of those goals, I have to help you achieve the specific *objectives* related to each goal. Because the goals and objectives are stated in proper form, they will name what *you, the reader/learner,* should be able to do.

After reading this chapter you should be able to:

Goal 1: Define and relate three terms that name your intentions for instruction.

- Objective 1: Define three terms that name your intentions for instruction.

- Objective 2: Explain the relationship between terms that name your intentions for instruction.

Goal 2: Write instructional goals that direct the learning/teaching activity.

- Objective 1: Define *instructional goal* in your own words.

- Objective 2: Explain six criteria for selecting an instructional goal.

- Objective 3: Apply three characteristics of a well-written goal to your goal statements.

Goal 3: Do a task analysis on an outcome or goal to generate logical, related subordinate learning requirements.

- Objective 1: Define *task analysis* in your own words.

- Objective 2: Do a task analysis on any behavior you want to teach.

- Objective 3: Give one justification for doing a task analysis on an intended outcome or goal.

- Objective 4: Name two types of task analysis and state the difference between them.

- Objective 5: Select the appropriate form of task analysis for any behavior you want to teach.

Goal 4: Write instructional objectives that add precision to teaching/learning activities.

- Objective 1: Define *instructional objective* in your own words.

- Objective 2: Explain the relationship between goals and objectives.

- Objective 3: Apply three characteristics of a well-written instructional objective to your instructional objectives.

This delineation of the relationship between the outcome, its related goals, and each of the goal's related objectives defines what you should learn by reading this segment of the chapter and practicing the skills it presents. It also provides an illustration of how the three different levels of learning intentions relate to each other. To illustrate the process, I first identified and stated what this segment of the chapter is about and called it the outcome. Second, I analyzed that outcome to determine what subordinate behaviors are required to accomplish what my outcome says you can do if you successfully complete this chapter. Third, as clearly and unambiguously as I could, I stated each of those things as goals. I concluded that most people don't have the knowledge or skills to achieve those four goals, so I analyzed each goal to identify what subordinate behaviors are required to achieve that goal. The behaviors I identified with my task analysis then became the instructional objectives.

What I am doing with this chapter is the same thing any teacher must do when designing a course. Before deciding what to include and what to exclude in this chapter, I had to create a rationale for doing both. Teachers must do this as well. They must clearly define and state the result, outcomes, goals, and objectives that will provide a roadmap for creating assignments, preparing class sessions, and writing quizzes and exams. Everything should be driven by what it contributes to a student's ability to learn one of these specific instructional objectives.

The following section is an explanation of how to create and write the result, outcomes, goals, and objectives for a course. Remember that the *outcome* of this section of the chapter is that by the time you have finished studying it you will be able to define and state instructional intentions that help you teach in a way that students actually learn what you intend at the level you intended.

It bears repeating that the following goals are stated in terms that identify what *you* the reader/student will be able to do and not what I as the teacher/writer intend to do. This is such a crucial point in designing instruction that it is difficult to overstate it. Only after clearly describing what students will do to demonstrate learning can teachers make good decisions about the methods they will use to help them learn.

GOAL 1: DEFINE AND RELATE THE FOUR TERMS THAT NAME
YOUR INTENTIONS FOR INSTRUCTION

Objective 1: Define the four terms that name your intentions for instruction

There are four terms to describe what you want students to know and do by the end of your course. Each term describes what the course, the sections of the course, the individual class session in the course, and the content of assignments and class activities in the course should help students achieve.

1. A *result* describes what the student can do when the *course* is finished.

2. *Outcomes* are more precise statements of tasks students must accomplish to achieve the course's *result* and normally relate to the course's sections.

3. *Goals* are more precise statements of tasks students must accomplish to achieve each *outcome*. *Goals* normally describe what should happen in one or a few class sessions.

4. *Objectives* are more precise statements of tasks students must accomplish to achieve each *goal*. *Objectives* describe what students will learn through assignments and class activities.

ILLUSTRATION

If the outcome is, "Write a term paper," there will be (at least) three goals:

1. Define the topic.

2. Research the topic.

3. Write the paper.

Two objectives for goal #2, "Research the topic," could be:

1. Use a library.

2. Use the internet.

Objective 2: Explain the relationship between the four terms that describe your intentions for instruction

The relationship between the four terms that describe instructional intentions is hierarchical because each set of statements describes what learners must do to achieve the next higher level. *Outcomes* describe what students will do to achieve *results*. *Goals* describe what students must do to achieve the *outcomes*. *Objectives* describe what students must do to achieve the *goals*. You can analyze the operative verb in each statement to generate the next lower level of statements.

For example, a parent can analyze a result as simple as brushing teeth and generate the result into outcomes, goals, and objectives for a young child who has never brushed his teeth before:

The *result* is to have healthy teeth and gums.

The *outcome* is to properly "brush your teeth."

The *goals* are to:

1. find the toothbrush

2. find the toothpaste

3.   put toothpaste on the toothbrush

4.   put the toothbrush in your mouth and brush

Analyzing goals 1 and 2 might determine that no further explanation is needed, in which case there would be no need to write objectives.

However, goal 3—"Put toothpaste on the toothbrush"—could result in a disastrous mess in the bathroom without some instruction, since the student is a child. So, the parent could write the following objectives for goal 3:

1.   Take the lid off the tube.

2.   Squeeze the tube (better include further instruction here).

3.   Cover the toothbrush bristles with toothpaste (a bit more instruction here).

When analyzing goal 4, parents may conclude they need to consult a dentist to learn about the most effective way to brush teeth.

Adults are so familiar with brushing teeth that they face the danger of leaving steps out and frustrating the learner—and creating a mess. Likewise, those who preach regularly may overlook important steps in the process of preparing and preaching a sermon. How troubling would it be if a student was given a low grade on their sermon because they didn't include an introduction—when the teacher forgot to teach introductions?

GOAL 2: WRITE INSTRUCTIONAL GOALS THAT DIRECT THE
LEARNING/TEACHING ACTIVITY

Objective 1: Define instructional goal in your own words

An instructional goal describes what students will do to demonstrate their level of success in learning.

Objective 2: Explain five criteria for selecting an instructional goal

A frequent frustration in designing a course is the lack of time to teach everything at the level you want to teach it. So, you must make some hard decisions about what goals must be included. You must ask the simple question, "Is there a need for this goal?" followed by, "Have they already studied it?" "Is this the most pressing need?" and "Is it necessary or is it just a 'nice' addition?" Teachers must avoid teaching things simply because they like to teach them.

If you have identified the goal as essential, make sure you are competent to teach it. If not, ask yourself if you can get up to speed in the time available to be prepared to teach it. Should you invite a consultant? If you have discovered through analyzing your outcome that eliminating this goal is not an option, you need to make some decisions about how you will teach it.

Sometimes a goal may be stated in such a way that there isn't time to cover it. Ask yourself if you should move it to a more advanced course or an elective. Is there another goal of lesser importance that you can give less time to so you can steal time for this one? Are you going more deeply into this goal than you need to?

Be certain that the goals address major trouble spots. Did you adequately cover the tough parts of the outcome statement? What parts need skill practice or multiple sessions or additional homework? Will this goal raise fear or frustration in students and require extra time and motivation?

Ask if the verb in the goal is the right one. Does it equip students to succeed only in class, or does it relate to their referent situation? The danger is students becoming well equipped to succeed in class at the expense of being equipped to function in their real world. Examine your goals to be sure they are anchored in reality.

Objective 3: Apply three characteristics of a well-written goal to your goal statements

A well-written goal is one that both student and teacher can observe and recognize as successful or unsuccessful. You can help yourself design more helpful course material and thereby help your students achieve what the course was designed to accomplish when you write clear instructional goals.

To be well written, a goal must first contain an observable behavior. It is true of both goals and objectives that the more easily students can observe themselves performing what the goal asks for, the more helpful that goal is. Students can focus on a clearly stated behavior they are expected to perform to demonstrate how well they have learned what the goal asks from them. Teachers can design more precise learning experiences that zero in on what students must know and do to achieve the goal. This will allow teachers to grade students' work with greater objectivity, precision, and, consequently, fairness.

Second, a good goal is sized to the learner's need. Given the amount of time you can devote to this goal, is your statement over- or understated? Is it appropriate for the grade level this course is designed for? Is it large enough to keep students motivated and challenged? Is it so aggressive they will become frustrated and anxious? Is there room for individual pacing for students who want to pursue it further?

Third, a good goal must be stated in clear, understandable language. Are you using terms with ambiguous meaning (i.e., "well-rounded" or "impactful"), or that students may not understand (i.e., "sanctified" or "justified"), or that are hard to measure (i.e., "committed" or "full-fledged")? Sometimes expertise in a field works against us. We forget that over the years we have developed a vocabulary that is strange to students who are entering our field of expertise.

GOAL 3: DO A SIMPLE TASK ANALYSIS ON A RESULT, AN OUTCOME, AND A GOAL STATEMENT TO GENERATE LOGICALLY RELATED SUBORDINATE LEARNING INTENTIONS

A task analysis is a procedure that identifies behaviors required to complete a task. To complete a task analysis, you must mentally—or physically—walk step by step through the procedure you want to teach. In the toothpaste illustration, you "analyzed" a process you have completed so many times that you do it without thinking of the individual steps involved. Similarly, after writing a number of sermon introductions, you may forget the mechanics of what to include in a good introduction. At this point in designing your course, you'll need to pretend you have never written an introduction and review the process at its most basic level. You may have to check your homiletics text again to refresh your memory of what an introduction should include.

You may do a task analysis by yourself or with another person who has expertise in the task you are analyzing. All you need to do is think through the task step by step and make sure you haven't left a step out of the process.

The objectives for this goal are:

1.   Define *task analysis* in your own words.

2. List the steps required to perform a task analysis on any behavior you want to teach.

3. Give one justification for doing a task analysis on an intended result, outcome, or goal.

4. Name two types of task analysis and state the difference between them.

5. Select the appropriate form of task analysis for any behavior you want to teach.

Objective 1: Define task analysis

A task analysis is a procedure that, when applied to an instructional result, outcome, or goal, identifies relevant subordinate skills required to achieve that result, outcome, or goal.[2]

Objective 2: List the steps required to perform a task analysis on any behavior you want to teach

Four steps are required to complete a task analysis. First, state what you want the student to learn. It is impossible to analyze the task if you haven't clearly decided what the task is. Then, identify subordinate skills needed to achieve the behavior you have named. Ask yourself what steps that behavior requires for a person to complete it. When writing an introduction, for instance, I know that a good introduction has to focus listeners' attention on the idea of the biblical text I plan to preach on. Second, it has to generate interest in the idea. And third, it has to move logically into the biblical text. If—when preparing a class session on introductions—I fail to address any of these three skills, my students will not know how to prepare a good introduction. The time invested in analyzing the goal "Write an introduction" helps to generate and write goals and objectives that help prepare an effective class on introductions.

Next, organize the subordinate skills in sequential order when appropriate. Asking students to outline their sermon before they have completed

---

2. A relevant subordinate skill is one that, although not necessarily important as an isolated skill, must be achieved to accomplish a super-ordinate skill.

their exegesis will only frustrate their attempt. They have to know the details of the passage before they can outline it. A child can't put toothpaste on a toothbrush if she hasn't taken the lid off the toothpaste tube first. On the other hand, a student may write the section of their introduction that addresses the need for the idea before they write the section on how to draw listeners' attention to the idea. If the tasks must be completed in sequence, make that clear and teach them in proper sequence.

Finally, draw either a procedural or hierarchical task analysis diagram. These two kinds of diagrams are explained in objective four, following the illustration of a task analysis.

Here's an illustration of a task analysis on each level of instructional intentions:

Result = What the course will enable learners to do:
Prepare and preach an effective sermon
Doing a task analysis on that result produces three …

Outcomes = What learners must be able to do to realize the course results. Usually these become the course units:
1. *Identify and exegete a preaching text*
2. *Craft that text into a sermon*
3. *Preach the sermon*
Doing a task analysis on outcome #2, "Craft that text into a sermon," produces three …

Goals = What learners must do to achieve the outcomes. Usually these are attached to individual sessions:
1. *Write an introduction*
2. *Prepare the body of the sermon*
3. *Write a conclusion*
Doing a task analysis on goal #1, "Write an introduction," produces three …

> **Objectives** = What learners must do to achieve the goals. The most specific statements of instructional intentions, these become the outline you follow as you design each class session.
>
> 1. *Gain attention to the sermon idea*
>
> 2. *Generate interest in the sermon idea*
>
> 3. *Move the listeners logically into the biblical text*
>
> Or **Attention/Interest/ Movement** = **AIM** your audience at the sermon idea in your text.

Objective 3: Justify using a task analysis

Use a task analysis to avoid overlooking steps essential to completing the task or adding unneeded steps that confuse students.

Objective 4: Name two types of task analysis and state the difference between them

The two types of task analysis are *procedural* and *hierarchical*. There is a simple but important difference between the two.

In a *procedural task analysis*, the behavior to be taught is a series of acts that must be performed in sequence and needs no further instruction for the student to complete. A procedural task analysis might be to find John 10:10 in the Bible.

Identify the passage	Go to the table of contents	Locate the page number for John's Gospel	Turn to John	Find chapter 10	Find verse 10

Assuming no students need to be taught any of these skills, you can therefore teach each goal in a linear fashion.

In a *hierarchical task analysis*, the behavior to be taught contains subordinate skills that students cannot perform without additional instruction. A hierarchical task analysis might be to conduct the Observation Step of Inductive Bible Study on John 10:10.

Observation					Interpreta-tion	Applica-tion
Define "Who"	Define "What"	Define "Where"	Define "When"	Define "How"	Etc.	Etc.

I am assuming students will not know how to do any of the three steps of observation, interpretation, or application when they attempt to do an inductive study of a Bible passage. So I ask what a person "does" when they "Observe," "Interpret," or "Apply" a biblical text. In the illustration above I generated five skills I have to teach students if I expect them to "Observe" a biblical text.

If I leave a step out of the process, students can't complete the task and get discouraged. If I include unnecessary steps, students become overwhelmed by irrelevant information and become frustrated.

Objective 5: Select the appropriate form of task analysis for any behavior you want to teach

The type of analysis you will use depends entirely on the nature of the behavior in the goal. If it is impossible for students to complete one subordinate skill without first learning an enabling skill, the analysis is hierarchical. Otherwise it is procedural.

GOAL 4: WRITE INSTRUCTIONAL OBJECTIVES THAT ADD
PRECISION TO TEACHING/LEARNING ACTIVITIES

The objectives for this goal are:

1. Define *instructional objective* in your own words.

2. Explain the relationship between goals and objectives.

3. Apply three characteristics of a well-written instructional objective to your instructional objectives.

Objective 1: Define instructional objective *in your own words*

An instructional objective is a statement that *describes* an intended outcome of instruction that can be recognized as successful or unsuccessful by both students and teacher.

For an objective to be recognized as successful or unsuccessful, both the student and the teacher must be able to see it and measure it. Therefore, objectives must be stated in behavioral terms. If the verb in the objective is "know," ask how students will demonstrate that they "know." If you use more precise and behavioral terms like "list," "describe," "reproduce," or "match," you can "see" students perform. Students know exactly what they must do to demonstrate learning, and both you and the student can see if their response matched the objective.

Objective 2: Explain the relationship between a goal and its objectives

The relationship between a goal and an objective is simple but important. A goal is a broader statement of intent, and an objective is a more precise statement that logically grows out of a task analysis of the main verb in the goal. Because a goal normally has more than one objective associated with it, and its objectives list the more precise behaviors students must perform to accomplish that goal, use a task analysis to make sure that you have sufficient objectives for each goal and that you don't have nonessential objectives that overly complicate the task.

When all of the objectives related to a goal are added together they must equal the goal:

objective 1 + objective 2 + objective 3 = the goal

When all of the objectives related to a goal are added together and there is a nonessential object included, eliminate the nonessential ones.

objective 1 + objective 2 + objective 3 + ~~objective 4~~ = the goal

If any required subordinate behavior is missing, add it as another objective statement. If any unneeded objectives are included, eliminate them, or students' time will be wasted and the lesson will be confusing.

Objective 3: Apply three characteristics of a well-written instructional objective

An objective must name the terminal behavior in specific enough terms that both student and teacher can observe and measure it. Ambiguous terms like "know," "understand," and "appreciate" don't work in stating objectives (or goals) because neither the student nor the teacher can clearly see if the student has successfully learned. Consequently, the student can neither enjoy the success of achievement nor identify what they haven't "learned" so they can invest the additional attention needed to learn it.

When writing both goals and objectives, it is also important to review learning levels and include verbs that address more complex learning levels. If you only write objectives that require listing items or repeating definitions—as essential as those learning levels are—you have short-changed your students. You must also include objectives with verbs that require students to analyze, explain, defend, and create so students accomplish more technical levels of learning. The following table illustrates the difference between non-behavioral and behavioral terms and lists verbs that represent various learning levels:

Do **not** say students will ...	*Instead*, say students will ...
know	list, define, select
comprehend	defend, explain
be able to do	operate, compute, use
understand	diagram, select, outline
value or appreciate	prioritize, describe, explain, select
realize	create, write, draw, construct

It is important to describe the conditions under which the student will be expected to demonstrate learning. You help your students prepare for exams and presentations, and more importantly for their real-world experience, when your objectives state how they will be asked to demonstrate learning. Will students be allowed to use books on an exam? Will they give a speech before the whole class or a small group? Can they use notes when they preach?

If students are not clear about how they will be expected to demonstrate what they have learned, they may feel cheated. If they prepared for an objective exam and you give an essay exam, or if they prepared to preach their sermon with notes and you don't allow them to use the notes, they will justifiably feel they have been treated unfairly.

Objectives should also state the standard of performance related to each level of success. When applying Bloom's learning levels to your objectives, you can itemize how far up Bloom's level of expertise you expect a student to perform on each objective. Some things must be memorized word-for-word and others not. Some lists may require students to produce ten of the ten items, while others do not. Some things need to be listed in a certain order, some not, etc. Decide if you want a paper to include extensive documentation or a performance to meet certain specific criteria, and state that in your objectives. A well-written objective tells students what level of performance will earn them an A, a B, and so on.

CONCLUSION

The time you invest in the meticulous process of identifying and clearly articulating what students must do to demonstrate success in your course will be redeemed when you prepare and teach your class sessions and when you issue grades to students. But the greatest payback comes when students demonstrate how well they have learned the knowledge, skills, and attitudes you *intentionally* helped them learn.

9

○ ○ ○

The Value of Feedback: Speaking the Truth in Love

CHRIS RAPPAZINI

Feedback is the breakfast of champions.[1]

If you are reading this book, you already know that words are powerful. They have the ability to build someone up or to tear someone down. They can leave impressions on people's lives that can last a lifetime. I can still recall several crucial instances in my life where the words people used made all the difference for me. Likewise, the feedback you give students has the potential to transform lives. It can hinder someone from God's calling, or it can ignite a passion in someone's heart that could change the trajectory of their life forever.

Some of your students will soon be moving on to lead churches or ministries, and feedback needs to be part of their DNA. As a professor of preaching you have the ability to teach your students the incredible value of both giving and receiving feedback.

I encourage you to think of feedback as a significant component of the overall learning process. Dennis Phelps, from New Orleans Baptist Theological Seminary, says that feedback is beneficial in "helping the student grow in the ability to listen and think more objectively, critically, and practically about how to improve their own preaching in order to grow personally and professionally in the years ahead."[2] As part of your pedagogy, feedback will enhance your students' experiences because it will cause them to reflect and hopefully grow in their preaching ability and character.

---

1. Ken Blanchard, *Leading at a Higher Level: Blanchard on Leadership and Creating High Performing Organizations*, rev. ed. (Upper Saddle River, NJ: BMC, 2010), 133.

2. Dennis Phelps, email message to author, November 14, 2015.

Carol S. Dweck, author of *Mindset,* expresses the importance of growth when she writes, "The great teachers believe in the growth of the intellect and talent, and they are fascinated with the process of learning."[3] One of the most beneficial ways a student can grow is through effective feedback.

To gain a comprehensive idea of various forms of feedback, I solicited several syllabi, preaching forms, and sermon rubrics from multiple veteran professors of preaching at Bible colleges, seminaries, and graduate schools across the country.[4] There was an overwhelming consensus that following the weeks of lectures, students should be given the opportunity to implement the course material through the development and delivery of their own sermons, which should then be followed by written and oral feedback. This chapter explores various ways that feedback enhances the learning process by laying a foundation for preparing students to thrive in a culture of feedback and suggesting action steps to take when conveying and contributing detailed feedback. It then addresses and answers some questions and concerns regarding feedback that will arise during your first few years of teaching the subject of preaching.

CULTIVATING A CULTURE OF FEEDBACK

PREPARING FOR FEEDBACK FROM DAY ONE

It is tempting to think that feedback does not start until after the first assignment is completed. Actually, there is much groundwork for eventual feedback that needs to be laid beforehand. Every successful crop farmer knows that fertile soil is essential for good growth; likewise, to give effective feedback you must prepare the ground for students to develop into communicators. One advantage you have in teaching a preaching class is the ability to leverage your own experiences as a student. At one point in

---

3. Carol S. Dweck, *Mindset: The New Psychology of Success* (New York: Ballantine, 2006), 194.

4. Course syllabi, grading rubrics, and an answer to the prompt, "What is the most effective thing you do when giving oral or written feedback?" were collected from Dr. Jared Alcántara, Baylor's Truett Theological Seminary; Dr. David Allen, Southwestern Baptist Theological Seminary; Dr. Kenton Anderson, Associated Canadian Theological Schools; Dr. Jeffery Arthurs, Gordon-Conwell Theological Seminary; Dr. Scott Gibson, Baylor's Truett Theological Seminary; Dr. Daniel Green, Moody Theological Seminary; Dr. John Koessler, Moody Bible Institute; Dr. Rock LaGioia, Grace Theological Seminary; Dr. Dennis Phelps, New Orleans Baptist Theological Seminary; and Dr. Don Sunukjian, Talbot School of Theology.

your educational experience, you were most likely sitting in a similar situation as that of your students. You were nervous to preach, anxious to hear what your professor thought of your work, and possibly intimidated by other students in the class. From day one, do not hesitate to share your personal experiences. This vulnerability will aid in creating a safe and healthy culture, and you will likely cultivate rapport with your students.

Facilitating a safe learning environment is crucial for feedback to be effective. It is important for students to know from the beginning of the semester that the classroom is a laboratory and a place to stretch and grow. When establishing a learning community in your classroom, Jere Brophy writes, "You will need to establish and maintain your classroom as a learning community—a place where students come primarily to learn, and succeed in doing so through collaboration with you and their classmates."[5] Your class is one of the few times in their academic career where others will speak truth into students' lives and they will have the opportunity to do the same into the lives of their peers. I often tell students that we are all on the journey together and that I am just as excited to learn from them as I am about teaching the material.

Feedback coming from any professor can be appreciated, but when a student senses the professor truly cares for him or her, the feedback can be priceless. Your class is one of the smallest size classes your students will be part of throughout their education. In these smaller classes, it is crucial to recall students' names and be familiar with them individually. Sidney Greidanus, former preaching professor at Calvin Theological Seminary, would go the extra mile and meet with every student for ten minutes at the beginning of the semester simply to get to know each student better. He would "write on a 3 x 5 card the name of the student, married status, number of children, home town, denominational affiliation, college attended, speech courses taken, former occupation, and any concerns the student may have about preaching."[6] He credited this small interaction as helping build rapport with students and enhancing classroom

---

5. Jere Brophy, *Motivating Students to Learn*, 3rd ed. (New York: Routledge, 2010).

6. Sidney Greidanus, "Teaching First-Year Preaching" (paper presented at the annual meeting for the Evangelical Homiletics Society: Preparing Those Who Preach, Vancouver, BC, October 16–18, 2003).

discussions. Personal feedback will often be better received if students recognize that their professor cares about them personally.

TEACHING STUDENTS WHAT EFFECTIVE FEEDBACK IS AND HOW TO COMMUNICATE IT

Students often do not know what effective feedback looks like. It is a skill rarely taught in other classes; therefore, it will be helpful to teach your students how to give valid critiques. Remember, you are teaching students not only how to preach but also how to be active listeners and mature leaders for their future churches and ministries. Here are three ways you can assist in teaching them how to contribute in giving effective feedback.

First, write on the whiteboard ineffective statements that hinder learning ("You had good illustrations," or "I did not like your delivery"). Then, have the class rewrite the critiques by being more concrete and descriptive.[7] Many students have a difficult time expressing specifically what they mean in their evaluations, so teach them to include the word "because" in their feedback:

> You had a good introduction *because* through your personal story, listeners will be able to relate to your surfaced need of fear.

or,

> It seemed as if you had two main ideas *because* throughout much of the sermon you talked about grace but then in your conclusion you brought up justice.

Second, while lecturing, show a sermon clip of someone preaching (preferably not yourself). As a class, evaluate the sermon and point out its strengths and weaknesses. By using someone else's sermon, students can be more objective and not feel like they will be hurting a classmate's feelings.

Third, practice "feed-forward," and use their preparation process as a teachable moment. "Feed-forward" is giving valuable advice *before* students stand to preach. Scott Gibson, from Baylor's Truett Theological Seminary, has students turn in their outline two weeks before their first sermon. After

---

7. Deanna P. Dannels, *Eight Essential Questions Teachers Ask: A Guidebook for Communicating with Students* (New York: Oxford University Press, 2015), 185.

he returns the graded outlines, students then have the option of reworking them for a higher grade until a few days before they preach.[8] Since many students are motivated by their grade, this helps them earn a grade that they are satisfied with, teaches them what a correct outline looks like, and prevents procrastination. In smaller classes, you might have a workshop and evaluate each student's work together as a group, and then ask the class what changes they would make if it were their sermon.

Remember, you are preparing students not only for one sermon, but for a lifetime of communicating and listening to God's truth. Helping them learn how to give and receive solid feedback will benefit them in whatever position or role they find themselves. Once they experience the value of feedback in your classroom, they will hopefully crave it in other areas of their lives as well.

CONVEYING AND CONTRIBUTING FEEDBACK

VARIOUS ROLES OF GRADING

I have heard a phrase begrudgingly uttered throughout the halls of the faculty offices, "I love to teach. They pay me to grade." While grading can seem like a nuisance, I want to suggest that you view grading as an extension of your commitment to the student's learning process. When I first began teaching, I had a vague idea of what lecturing would be like and absolutely zero idea of what grading would look like. I knew I was supposed to grade, but what I did not know was *how* to grade. I eventually learned that there are several different roles in grading. Below are just a few of these grading roles:

1. Assessor: The teacher examines the work and responds by giving information on what will help the next time.

2. Mentor: The teacher seeks to understand the student's intentions and course of thinking by guiding them along in the process.

---

8. Scott M. Gibson, "Preaching: Principles and Practice in Preparing Relevant and Biblical Sermons, PR 601" (syllabus, Gordon-Conwell Theological Seminary, South Hamilton, MA, 2015).

3. Judge: The teacher evaluates the work from an objective point of view and remarks based solely on the content of the work and not on the student personally. The teacher seeks to give clear "right" or "wrong" answers.

4. Colleague: The teacher attempts to help the student as a co-participant in the work being done. The teacher provides more casual suggestions with the understanding that the work belongs to the student and they must make decisions on how to improve.

5. Coach: The teacher works to draw out the best out of each student both in academics and in character. This will involve challenging and encouraging when needed.[9]

Eventually, you will have to decide which role(s) is best suited for you. It is also essential to realize that even though you may naturally gravitate toward one role, your students may have a different preference. It is important to communicate to them which one of these roles you normally lean toward. This will allow them to filter your feedback through a specific lens.

WRITTEN AND ORAL FEEDBACK AFTER A SERMON

There are many ways to give feedback after the sermon, and my main suggestion is to figure out what works best for you and fulfills your course goals and objectives. Knowing that students are anxious about speaking in front of their peers, try to be as clear as possible regarding what they can expect when receiving both written and oral feedback. Remind them that there is no such thing as a perfect sermon and there is always room to grow.

Regarding written feedback, the class and I fill out a sermon grading rubric (see appendix 1) during the sermon, and the class gives their forms to the preacher at the end of the day. I tend to hold on to mine for a day to

---

9. Ervin R. Stutzman, "Toward Excellence in Equipping Preachers: Four Foci for Classroom Instruction" (paper presented at the annual meeting for the Evangelical Homiletics Society, South Hamilton, MA, October 12–14, 2006). See Dannels, *Eight Essential Questions Teachers Ask*, 16–172. Dannels adapted from C. M. Anson, "Writing and Response: Theory, Practice, and Research" (paper presented at National Council of Teachers of English, Urbana, IL, 1989) and J. Britton, "The Development of Writing Abilities" (paper presented at National Council of Teachers of English, Urbana, IL, 1975).

let the sermon sink in and allow the preacher to get over the adrenaline of having just preached in front of his or her peers. The sermon grading rubric that I use, which you are welcome to use and adjust, was compiled after reviewing other preaching professors' evaluation forms. There was a clear consensus from those forms that the following areas are to be observed and evaluated: Introduction, Biblical Accuracy, Clarity, Contemporary Relevance, Structure, Application/Conclusion, and Delivery.[10]

I'll admit, it is somewhat challenging assessing sermons and marking a grade since every sermon is uniquely different, and you are evaluating a skill/event as opposed to responses on a Hebrew or Greek exam. For instance, a student can excel on each element of the sermon yet it feels flat and uninspiring, while on the other hand, a student might be a mediocre speaker but the sermon really moved people in the room. This is why I have both quantitative and qualitative elements in my written feedback. There are numerical components as well as places to write my overall thoughts and suggestions. When it comes to giving a final grade, I hold off until after class and comprehensively consider the speaker, grading rubric, sermon quality, and classroom response, and then choose an appropriate letter grade.

Immediately after the sermon, however, I lead a classroom discussion and give the preacher oral feedback. I usually stay consistent and ask the following four questions. While I am aware that there are many ways to give post-sermon feedback, here is a suggestion of prompts one could ask:

1. Now that you are finished, how do you feel it went? (*directed toward preacher*)

2. What do you think were the strongest parts of his or her sermon? (*directed toward entire class*)

3. What areas did you want to hear more of, or less of? What parts could be improved, and how? (*directed toward entire class*)

4. Do you have any advice for your classmates on what you would have done differently? (*directed toward preacher*)

---

10. Collection of grading rubrics from Bible colleges, seminaries, and graduate schools.

Now That You Are Finished, How Do You Feel It Went?

The student who finished preaching has been amped up and anticipated this sermon for days, perhaps weeks. Now that it is over, the student is still running off of adrenaline and the sermon high. I ask this question to allow the student to get anything off his or her chest before the class gives their feedback. Sometimes the student already knows what worked well or what did not. When each student can identify his or her own strengths and weaknesses, he or she is growing as a communicator. By giving the student an opportunity to answer this question, it enables them to hear the feedback from the rest of the class and receive it with openness and a willingness to learn. I often conclude this question by asking something like, "Is it okay if we give you some of our thoughts?" By asking and getting permission from the student to receive feedback, he or she is inviting critiques and may be more receptive to them after having granted approval.

What Do You Think Were the Strongest Parts of This Sermon?

This question is directed toward the class and is their time to encourage the preacher. I will often echo what has been said and give my thoughts on the best parts of the sermon. There will always be something you can find in a sermon that the student did well. At the end of this question I will usually conclude by clearly summarizing what I thought was the sermon's strongest part(s). Remember to use any portion of the feedback as a teachable moment. Strive to make your feedback reinforce what was previously taught in the lectures and class readings.

What Areas Did You Want to Hear More of, or Less of? What Parts Could Be Improved, and How?

This is the part of the evaluation process that the student is dreading the most. The student knows it is coming and sometimes does not even absorb all the positive comments just spoken because he or she is focused on anticipating the critiques. It is always a good idea to remind students why this portion of the feedback is necessary and valuable—even if this means mentioning, for example, "Now remember, we want to sharpen one another, not tear each other down. Jacki might have the opportunity to give this message when she is home for break, so let's give her some productive advice." I never want to "burn" or embarrass anyone during the feedback process, so I often use Jim Collins's language and ask, "What would help make this sermon go from a good sermon to a great sermon?"[11] This reinforces the student's efforts but reminds everyone that there is always room to grow.

In this portion of the feedback, I again let the students share but interject to agree or disagree after each comment. Many preaching professors use this time to give concrete examples of what could have been done to improve aspects of the sermon. Students will gain the most learning from more detailed examples. Do not only point out parts that need to be improved; go the next step and show them what you mean. Say things like, "If you were to preach this sermon again, maybe you could say... " and then give them a tangible example. If you are ever at a loss for words, ask yourself, "If it were my sermon, how would I do things differently?" Although you may be new to teaching, you are still the most qualified and experienced person in the room. Give them a glimpse of what could have made their sermon even better. Be confident because you are their mentor, coach, counselor, and assessor. Reintroduce the language you used earlier.

Do You Have Any Advice for Your Classmates on What You Would Have Done Differently?

This final question is crucial. It allows the student to share what he or she has learned from the experience and usually gives valuable advice to fellow classmates. Suggestions shared are often similar to, "I should have probably started working on my sermon a lot sooner," or, "I was nervous at first but once I got going it seemed more natural." Most likely you have already expressed the same words of wisdom to the class, but when they hear it from a fellow classmate it adds another layer of credibility to the learning experience.

Another teaching technique that is fairly consistent in many preaching classes is recording the sermon. This gives the student an opportunity to view himself or herself preaching the sermon later and identify areas

---

11. Jim Collins, *Good to Great: Why Some Companies Make the Leap ... and Others Don't* (New York: HarperCollins, 2001).

that went well and other areas that need improvement. While at times this might be the most nauseating exercise for the student to bear, it can also be the most beneficial.

CURIOSITIES AND CONCERNS
ABOUT GIVING FEEDBACK

As you are finding your own voice and style as a professor, you may come across questions and concerns regarding grading and evaluation. In this section, I address a few issues and concerns you may have in your first few years:

1. What feedback should I give to a student who does poorly?

2. How do I respond to an argumentative student who challenges my grading?

3. What if another student gives feedback that is contrary to my feedback?

4. What if I find someone cheating through plagiarism or using notes when I require no notes?

WHAT FEEDBACK SHOULD I GIVE TO A STUDENT WHO DOES POORLY?

Pray. It sounds trite, but while the student is preaching and on your way to the front of the class, pray a quick prayer under your breath that the Lord will help the student and you. Remember that your goal is not to help the student pass the class with one or two good sermons in their back pocket. Your goal, as well as the student's goal, ought to be learning. I have heard many stories of the professor blistering a student with unconstructive words because of a poor preaching performance. Your goal is not to make a *point*—it is to make a *difference*.

Try directing more questions toward the preacher to see if he or she can pinpoint exactly what the problem was. Often the student will recognize his or her lack of preparation as a key reason why the sermon was so poor. Also, even if the sermon was an absolute disaster, find at least one or two things the student did well and give him or her hope for the future.

This is also where written feedback can play a crucial role. Since written feedback is exclusively between you and the student, you can put in writing words that may come across as humiliating if said in front of the entire class. For instance, you could write:

Dear Tim,

Your opening illustration really grabbed our attention and drew us in. However, after that story, the rest of the sermon was a bit unclear and you seemed lost. From my observations over the past few weeks, it appears you are not giving the time and attention this class demands. I see a lot of potential in you being a good speaker, but you seem to be either preoccupied or are relying on natural ability and not doing the hard work that is necessary. Don't waste this opportunity to grow. I hope to see more out of you in the future. Let me know how I can help.

Remember, your goal is not to criticize but to critique in love. Sometimes taking a little extra time to challenge a student to live up to his or her potential can start a spark in them that sets them on fire for the Lord and his work.

If it appears that the student has been working hard but the sermon was still poor, be sure to encourage them on their effort. For many, speaking in front of large groups does not come naturally. Remind them that what you are looking for is growth, not perfection. Maybe say something like, "When learning any new skill, two things are needed: hard work and time. You know how to put in the hard work; the only thing left is time, and that will come. I believe in you."

HOW DO I RESPOND TO AN ARGUMENTATIVE STUDENT WHO CHALLENGES MY GRADING?[12]

When this happens, try to not feel threatened, but rather energized that the student is concerned about his or her grade. (Those who do not care at all about their grades are the ones that I wonder about.) Nonetheless, be sure to give the student time to digest the grade after receiving it. Then after a day or two, you may want to respond through an email or a face-to-face

---

12. Dannels, *Eight Essential Questions Teachers Ask*, 187–88.

meeting. Ask the student to come prepared with something in writing that indicates the question(s) he or she may have. Also, if your instructions for the assignment are clear in the syllabus, be sure to refer back to it. You do not have to change someone's grade simply because they challenged you. Instead, use this time to further explain why they earned the grade that they did. Try to keep your language centered on the work and not your grading. Remember, students do not receive grades, they earn them. So focus on what the student could have done differently to earn a higher grade. Concerning grading, Drs. Barbara Walvoord and Virginia Anderson suggest that "the grade is a communication, and it must communicate to a person who can use it for learning. Our chief responsibility is to help this learner move forward. So think to yourself, 'What does this learner need from me at this time?' Then shape your comments accordingly."[13] If you feel that a grade does indeed need to be changed, that is fine. But be careful because word may spread and you will have three more emails asking for a grade change by the end of the week.

WHAT IF ANOTHER STUDENT GIVES FEEDBACK THAT IS CONTRARY TO MY FEEDBACK?

As will be the case, when you open feedback up to the class, some people will present feedback different than yours. Instead of trying to make your case as to why your view is correct and theirs is not, use this as an opportunity to teach students how to have a cordial conversation with someone who has an opposing view. Ask for clarification and further understanding and try to repeat their view in your own words. If their opinion does not hinder or contradict your teaching, identify it as personal preference. However, if it does contradict your position, feel free to invite further dialogue outside of class.

WHAT IF I FIND SOMEONE CHEATING THROUGH PLAGIARISM— OR USING NOTES WHEN I REQUIRE NO NOTES?

Cheating is ubiquitous. It happens on every campus and your classroom is not exempt. Your institution will have a clear policy on cheating, so be

---

13. Barbra E. Walvoord and Virginia Johnson Anderson, *Effective Grading: A Tool for Learning and Assessment* (San Francisco: Josey-Bass, 1998), 110.

sure to put that in your syllabus. If you suspect someone of cheating, I encourage you to meet with them one on one. You may want to include your department chair, academic dean, or a senior faculty member since you are new to this type of situation. Without using an accusatory tone, ask the student about their work and the process they went through. They should be able to answer in detail and with confidence. Then calmly and clearly explain your concerns and provide evidence. Ask the student for an explanation and proceed based on their response and also the wisdom gained from those in authority.

If you require no notes be used when preaching, it will be fairly obvious if a student uses them. If it is clearly explained in the syllabus that you require no notes, then it is similar to using notes on an exam. You have the option of taking points off, giving a zero, or giving them a second chance with a point reduction. Try to decide what would be best for the student's overall learning.

CONCLUSION

Feedback comes in all shapes and sizes, but without a doubt, it is necessary. It is at the heart of learning and can be the most influential moment in a student's life. It has the potential to alter someone's path in a direction that can help them be successful for the kingdom of God as well as extremely beneficial for the churches and ministries they lead. However, giving and receiving feedback is a daunting task, and the preaching professor should be guarded; pointing out imperfections and flaws can lead to a critical spirit. But remember, when Jesus came to this world, he came to tell people about their imperfections and flaws as well. The apostle John said that when Jesus came, he came "full of grace and truth" (John 1:14). In his book *Incarnate Leadership*, former Whitworth University president Bill Robinson discusses the importance of balancing both grace and truth. He writes, "Truth without grace is harsh, usually self-centered, and very un-Christlike. Grace without truth is deceptively permissive, often lazy, and equally un-Christlike. Good leaders communicate both grace and truth in love."[14] You ought to have a similar mindset when giving feedback. Ask yourself in every situation, "What is the best way to gracefully speak truth

---

14. Bill Robinson, *Incarnate Leadership* (Zondervan: Grand Rapids, 2009), 81.

into this student's life?" Spend your years finding the right balance between grace and truth, and you will start to see the value of feedback. By speaking the truth in love, you have the potential to help students grow and change their lives forever.

10

o o o

Teaching with Trajectory: Equipping Students for the Lifelong Journey of Learning to Preach

TIMOTHY BUSHFIELD

> *Education in order to accomplish its ends both*
> *for the individual learner and for society must*
> *be based upon experience—which is always the*
> *actual life-experience of some individual.*[1]

Learning to preach and learning to play the piano have much in common. As my children have been in piano lessons over the years, I've listened as they have learned the basics of piano theory; I have also enjoyed watching them build on that theory as their skills have improved. This much is clear about playing the piano: one can learn the basics in just a few years, but playing like a master takes a lifetime of intentional, dedicated practice. The best piano teachers are the ones who teach for both today and tomorrow: they teach today's lesson, and they also teach for tomorrow by instilling in each of their students a love for piano and a desire to keep learning.

A similar educational framework applies to preaching. The principles and theory of effective preaching can be learned in just a few seminary courses, but learning to preach with excellence takes a lifetime of intentional, dedicated practice. Teachers of preaching can equip their students with the tools needed to become great preachers—but *becoming* a great preacher lies well beyond the scope of what a typical seminary program can offer. Becoming a great preacher takes experience, and the vast majority of this experience happens not in the seminary classroom but in the

---

1. John Dewey, *Experience and Education* (New York: Touchstone, 1938), 89.

local church. Sally Ann Brown recognizes this when she acknowledges that "the sanctuary on Sunday morning, not the preaching classroom, is probably by far the more significant space of homiletical learning."[2] The best teachers of preaching, then, are the ones who teach for both today and tomorrow: they teach today's lesson, but they teach for tomorrow by instilling in students a love for preaching and equipping them with the tools they need to become lifelong learners in the practice.

Therefore, the comparison to playing the piano is apt: given the short time preaching teachers have with their students, they should not aim to manufacture fully-formed preachers any more than piano students could become fully-formed musicians after just a few years of lessons. In addition to teaching the principles and theory of effective preaching, preaching teachers also need to equip students with the tools they need to continue learning across the lifetime of experience that is yet to come. Preaching teachers need to be teaching with this trajectory in mind.

TEACHING WITH TRAJECTORY

Regardless of the specific discipline, it is good pedagogy to teach with an intentional focus on the future. Every discipline, from languages to biblical studies to theology to church history, hopes to instill in students a lifelong love of the subject matter. But preaching holds a unique place within the seminary curriculum, and the teaching of preaching presents distinct challenges to the educational process that make teaching with this future-focused trajectory especially important.

PREACHING IS A SKILL

Preaching is unique within the seminary curriculum because it is a skill that requires practice to achieve proficiency. Students who are successful in the other seminary disciplines, which employ more of a research-and-report framework, are not ensured success in the homiletical endeavor. Preaching blends many additional dimensions that need to be considered, including: public speaking skills and rhetoric; the differentiation between what is interesting and what is of first importance in a text; the

---

2. As quoted in Ronald Allen, "Is Preaching Taught or Caught? How Practitioners Learn," *Theological Education* 41, no. 1 (2005): 147.

interpersonal relationships involved in a local congregation; capturing and keeping interest based on the attention span (or lack thereof) in today's churches; and the clear presentation of an argument that can lead a group of people toward a common discovery. Preaching involves an element of real-time performance that breaks out of the pastor's study and necessitates face-to-face interaction with a congregation.

Preaching needs to be understood, then, as a constellation of actions and behaviors that are better termed "a practice," exploring by analogy its similarities to "law, medicine, and accounting, and perhaps even … sailing, gardening, cooking, playing baseball, and making music."[3] In the preceding examples, it takes time and practice to develop proficiency in each field because they are not just fields of study; they are activities that are performed. The same is true of preaching. Said another way, a student can be highly proficient in writing reports, papers, and the process of exegesis, but when faced with standing up in front of a group of people to proclaim clearly the word of God, success in these other disciplines is insufficient to guarantee them success as a preacher.

The skill of preaching, however, does demand full proficiency across the spectrum of seminary disciplines because of its integrative nature. Ron Allen writes that preaching is unique "because it brings together the various theological disciplines in a way that is unlike almost any other sector of theological education."[4] Preaching requires an ability to integrate biblical studies with church history and theology, and to bring together pastoral ministry with counseling and church leadership to proclaim truth with efficacy to a community. Not surprisingly, this integration is a skill that requires ongoing opportunities for development.

A study exploring how preachers learn, funded by the Lilly Endowment in 2001, revealed what is intuitively well known among preachers: that, among other factors, "preaching every week in a parish, especially in the early years of ministry, [is] a setting in which their approach to preaching

---

3. Thomas G. Long and Leonora Tubbs Tisdale, eds., *Teaching Preaching as a Christian Practice: A New Approach to Homiletical Pedagogy* (Louisville, KY: Westminster John Knox Press, 2008), 5.

4. Allen, "Is Preaching Taught or Caught?" 146.

came into focus and maturity."[5] To become a great preacher, one must preach. It takes time to develop the skill of preaching. The limited number of classes in seminary is simply insufficient for developing the kind of proficiency teachers hope to someday see in their students.

FINDING ONE'S VOICE

There is a wondrous diversity of styles and approaches that can be employed for any given sermon. Some preachers prefer inductive sermons, others deductive. Some preach with more of a narrative flow; others preach more propositionally. Some engage in apologetics, while others spend more time dealing with the inner realities of the human heart. New preachers need time to discover where their proficiencies lie, and what approach allows them to present a sermon most effectively. It can take years for newly minted preachers to discover their voice—their own approach to preaching that leverages their unique gifts, temperament, and personality—for the homiletical task.

A few caveats are necessary here. The text comes first in shaping a sermon: any given sermon should employ a form and approach that is derived from the biblical text and that is best suited for communicating its central idea most clearly. Additionally, these various styles and approaches can and sometimes should all be incorporated into a single sermon. For example, a sermon may have a propositional element where a text is explained before an exhortative element where the text is applied. Likewise, a sermon may have an inductive component that leads to an assertion, which is followed by a deductive component that unpacks its significance. But it should also be recognized, and even celebrated, that some preachers are naturally gifted for some of these aspects more than others. Some preachers are natural storytellers, while others can unpack difficult theological concepts with clarity. It is appropriate for preachers to develop their own unique voice.

---

5. Allen, "Is Preaching Taught or Caught?" 146. Ironically, based on the same data, Allen draws the opposite conclusion to the one presented here. He argues that seminary students don't need more courses in preaching, but rather more courses in the classical theological disciplines of Bible, Christian tradition, systematic theology, and ethics, along with a corresponding emphasis on critical theological reflection. Later in his discussion, however, he draws attention to the integrative nature of preaching and its uniqueness within the seminary curriculum.

Many new preachers begin this development by listening to great sermons and great preachers.[6] They experiment by employing techniques and approaches that are derived from their preaching heroes, whether those heroes are preaching professors, nationally recognized celebrity preachers, or even the pastors students have grown up under. But becoming a great preacher doesn't happen by simply imitating one's heroes; it happens by discovering which style and approach is most consistent with the preacher God has created each one to be. This takes experimentation and creativity; it involves taking risks, testing new approaches, and trying on different styles.

But there does come a point when preachers settle on an identity and discover their voice. Kevin DeYoung offers this estimate: "Since 2002, the year I was ordained, I estimate that I've preached almost 500 times ... and I think it took about 450 sermons to find my voice."[7] Becoming a great preacher is a gradual process that allows—and should allow—wide and varied experimentation with various preaching styles, structures, and approaches. Teachers of preaching need to appreciate this continuing development of new preachers and teach with a trajectory in mind that extends beyond a classroom or semester.

CONGREGATIONAL EXPERIENCE AND SPIRITUAL MATURITY

Good preachers know their people. Effectiveness in preaching grows as a preacher grows together with a congregation—something that is almost impossible to simulate in the seminary classroom or preaching lab. As pastors preach over their tenure at a church, they are living among people who are experiencing the joys and sorrows of life together. So, for example, while seminary teaches the principles behind effective illustrations, it takes knowing an actual church body to find illustrations that connect with this specific group of people and their life experiences. Knowing what they've lived through, and living through it with them, provides a localization of preaching that cannot be well simulated in a preaching lab.

---

6. Allen, "Is Preaching Taught or Caught?" 145.

7. Kevin DeYoung, "Learning to Be Yourself as a Preacher: From One Still Trying to Do That," *9Marks: Preaching and Theology*, June 12, 2014, accessed September 24, 2015, http://9marks. org/article/learning-to-be-yourself-as-a-preacher-from-one-still-trying-to-do-just-that/.

Proficiency in preaching, therefore, grows alongside one's participation in a local church or community of faith over time.

Good preachers also know themselves. Young preachers can be dynamic and even insightful, but life experience leads to maturity and wisdom. The sanctifying work of the Holy Spirit in preachers' own lives will contribute significantly to their development as preachers. For example, repentance from significant personal sin is hard to preach until it has been lived. It can be done apart from this personal, Spirit-led process of confession, repentance, and transformation, but it will lack the authenticity and power of firsthand experience. Likewise, it is hard to preach about contentment and joy unless one has first experienced this place of rest in one's own life. Living through seasons of personal suffering also deepen one's faith and thus deepen one's preaching. This sanctification in the life of the preacher cannot be manufactured in the seminary classroom, yet it is essential to becoming a great preacher.

Preaching is a skill that requires time and practice to develop. Finding one's voice as a preacher takes years as young pastors experiment and explore various styles and approaches to preaching. Shared congregational experience and personal spiritual maturity contribute significantly to effective preaching. It is clear from these examples that most of what is involved in the student's growing into a great preacher lies beyond the seminary classroom in the student's future years of ministry.

Teachers of preaching need to equip students with a set of tools and a framework for continuing to learn as they head out into life and ministry.

FOUNDATIONS FOR TEACHING
WITH TRAJECTORY

To teach with this future trajectory in mind, teachers of preaching need to first envision what future learning will look like once students graduate, and then develop and teach a framework that can be applied during these upcoming years of self-directed learning. Educational theory provides an important foundation for teaching with trajectory, not just in the classroom, but outside the classroom as teachers strive to equip students to become lifelong learners. The works of David Kolb in experiential learning theory and Etienne Wenger in social learning theory are both instrumental in helping teachers of preaching think concretely about educational frameworks that will equip students for the future-based locus of their educational process.

David Kolb's main contribution to the continuing education of the preacher is the gift of *intentionality*.

Considering that 90 percent of churches around the world have less than two hundred people and are led by solo pastors,[8] the majority of seminary students who intend to pursue pastoral ministry (should they find employment as a pastor at all) will find themselves as the primary preacher for a local congregation. As a solo pastor, the sheer number of preaching cycles that occur Sunday after Sunday in these early years of ministry will undoubtedly shape a preacher. Too often, however, this learning happens accidentally, unintentionally, or by trial-and-error as new preachers struggle to keep up with all the other demands of the ministry. Yet this weekly preaching cycle is perfectly positioned for the application of experiential learning theory and for capturing the learning potential of these early years.

The experiential learning cycle as proposed by Kolb involves four classic elements: concrete experience, reflective observation, abstract conceptualization, and active experimentation, as seen in figure 10.1.[9]

Preachers can apply this cycle to their own preaching experience to be intentional about capturing the educational potential of this weekly rhythm. Consider the application of this cycle to the rhythms of preaching. Starting with *concrete experience*, preachers have a repeating context every single week from which learning can take place if some intentionality is brought to bear upon it. But too often, having preached a sermon, the pressures of life and ministry drive out any further intentional movement through the experiential learning cycle. Having survived last Sunday's sermon, the preacher runs headlong toward the coming Sunday with little

8. Karl Vaters, "9 No-Fault, No-Excuse Reasons Many Healthy Churches Stay Small," *Pivot: Innovative Leadership from a Small Church Perspective*, June 26, 2015, accessed October 22, 2015, http://www.christianitytoday.com/karl-vaters/2015/june/9-no-fault-no-excuse-reasons-many-healthy-churches-stay.html.

9. David A. Kolb, *Experiential Learning: Experience as the Source of Learning and Development* (Upper Saddle River, NJ: Pearson, 2014), 51.

reflection and even less time to revisit the experience and intentionally learn from it.

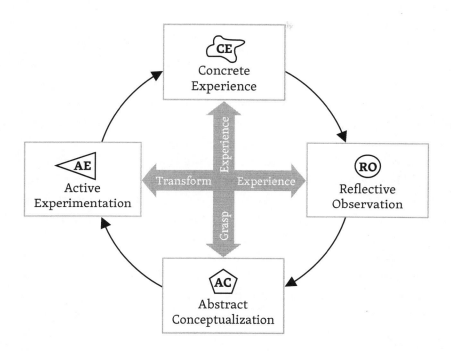

FIGURE 10.1. Kolb's Experiential Learning Cycle

But if Kolb's theory could be effectively applied, what would it look like to teach students in a way that not only equipped them to prepare a sermon, but also equipped them to process their own preaching experience and leverage it for ongoing personal growth? Application of the remaining three components of the experiential learning cycle would propel the weekly preaching rhythm beyond incidental learning toward purposeful growth.

Reflective observation is a challenge at the best of times for busy pastors. With so many demands on their time, slowing down to reflect on something that has already happened seems less than productive. But to avoid this reflection is to throw away valuable educational potential. A typical seminary class in preaching is heavily focused on the work that precedes the delivery of a sermon, with some additional emphasis on the actual delivery of the sermon. Preaching teachers might provide a comprehensive rubric for sermon evaluation, but do they equip students with questions that will help them notice what worked well—and what didn't? What tools do they offer students to help them evaluate their own sermons, and do they teach self-evaluation as an essential part of the sermon preparation process?

Consider also the role of *abstract conceptualization* in the experiential learning cycle. As preachers evaluate their sermons and reflect on their preaching, abstract conceptualization is the work of understanding their observations and generalizing them to a usable form of influence to affect the way they preach in the future. If preaching teachers do teach a post-sermon reflective process, they should also be giving students the tools they need to distill their observations into useful concepts they can use either as anchors in their preaching practice or as the basis for trying something new next time. Either way, preachers will only learn to the extent that they work through their observations and articulate them in a form that can influence a subsequent sermon.

Active experimentation is perhaps the climax of the experiential learning cycle. Because of the unrelenting nature of the weekly rhythm of preaching, pastors are perfectly positioned to apply creativity, innovation, and experimentation to their preaching. The sermon for a coming week can look intentionally different than the ones before it because the preacher is either refining effective practices or intentionally trying new approaches. The result is an upcoming sermon that will evidence reflective observation, abstract conceptualization, and active experimentation, all of which lead back in the cycle to concrete experience as the sermon is proclaimed that Sunday.

This learning cycle is perhaps better understood as a learning spiral, as Kolb himself proposes.[10] The ideal is that as students leverage the learning potential from these weekly preaching cycles, they will be accelerating their growth as preachers and moving closer to mastery with each pass through the cycle. The learning spiral provides an inherent trajectory that propels students toward becoming great preachers with increasing proficiency and confidence.

---

10. David A. Kolb, *Experiential Learning: Experience as the Source of Learning and Development* (Upper Saddle River, NJ: Pearson, 2014), 61.

However, there are criticisms of experiential learning theory. One such criticism is that Kolb's learning cycle is overly simplistic and that the learning process cannot be broken down into such discrete, identifiable steps. According to this argument, his cycle is a reductionist approach to experiential learning that cannot fully explain the holistic nature of learning from experience.[11] However, where experiential learning theory is being applied to preaching, this critique of the theory as a whole does not undermine its efficacy in the church. In fact, reductionism enables the identification of discrete steps that can be concretely implemented as a part of a preacher's repeating weekly rhythm of ministry—and this simplicity makes it useful for the preacher.

Teaching with trajectory means that teachers of preaching need to go beyond employing experiential learning theory in preaching labs. Teachers need to equip students with an understanding of experiential learning theory and teach a framework for its application in the local church as part of the preaching curriculum. Experiential learning theory offers growing practitioners the gift of *intentionality* in their efforts to become better preachers where so much of the deep learning happens—in the local church.

SOCIAL LEARNING THEORY

Etienne Wenger, an early voice in social learning theory, asked if learning had become too individualized. He counter-proposed that learning was best understood as a social phenomenon that occurred "in the context of our lived experience and participation in the world."[12] If Kolb offers growing preachers the gift of *intentionality*, Wenger's primary contribution is to highlight the importance of *community* as a necessary context for effective learning to take place. Preaching is not performed in isolation, but is a practice that legitimately and beautifully involves an entire community of faith or a congregation. Wenger coined the term "communities of practice"[13]

---

11. Jayson Seaman, "Experience, Reflect, Critique: The End of the 'Learning Cycles' Era." *Journal of Experiential Education*, 31 no. 1 (2008): 3–18.

12. Etienne Wenger, *Communities of Practice: Learning, Meaning, and Identity* (New York: Cambridge University Press, 1998), 3.

13. Wenger, *Communities of Practice*, xiii. Wenger shares the credit for coining this term with his colleague, Jean Lave.

and defined it as the social framework in which learning best takes place. Three dimensions constitute such a community: shared repertoire, joint enterprise, and mutual engagement, as seen in figure 10.2.[14]

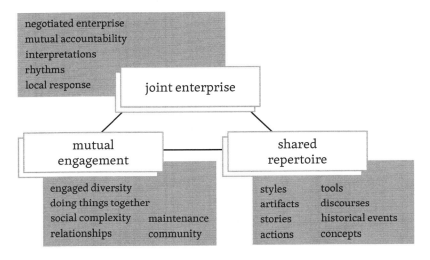

FIGURE 10.2. Wenger's Dimensions of Practice as a Property of a Community

The *shared repertoire* of a community of practice includes the rhythms, expectations, and ways of doing things that a community has adopted and to which meaning has been assigned. With respect to preaching specifically, this shared repertoire begins with an agreed-upon understanding of what constitutes effective preaching, but also extends to include expectations of who does the preaching, the duration of the sermon, and its placement in the worship service, as well as the various forms and structures of the sermons themselves together with the illustrations and rhetorical forms employed. A community of practice begins with a shared repertoire of parameters and elements that have been agreed upon, by intention or inheritance, by the community at large. The preacher is not alone in this practice; the congregation is deeply involved in the preacher's

---

14. Source: Etienne Wenger, *Communities of Practice: Learning, Meaning, and Identity* (New York: Cambridge University Press, 1998), 73.

social learning context by sharing in and, in some contexts, even directing the set of expectations that govern what is considered effective preaching.

Mutual engagement refers to the togetherness within a community of practice for accomplishing the larger goals of that community. The church's movement toward accomplishing its mission and vision involves a dynamic interplay between the broad diversity of participants (preachers and their congregations) as each part contributes to the whole, not unlike the body analogy employed in 1 Corinthians 12 and elsewhere in Scripture. The preacher may occupy a specialized role within that community, but not an isolated one. Instead, preaching is contributing to the larger goals of the church. As such, the preacher and the congregants are engaged together in working toward those larger goals, even while they carry different roles and responsibilities in the church. The preacher is therefore not alone in the practice of his or her craft, but rather employs his or her gifts in a social matrix of complex relationships that extend far beyond the act of preaching.

Joint enterprise presupposes the opportunity for participants in a specific practice to interact in meaningful ways. For a family, he explains, it may be having dinner together to debrief the day; in a company, it may be sharing an office space and talking over the water cooler about various problems and challenges. Joint enterprise implies that there is a group of fellow practitioners engaged together in working toward common goals.

Here lies a challenge to overcome: for the preacher, the idea of a joint enterprise, unlike the first two dimensions of a community of practice, is harder to find and even harder to create. For while it is readily acknowledged that preaching is a community-negotiated good with a shared repertoire and mutual engagement, preaching is also a specialized practice within a congregation. Few (if any) among a typical congregation are equipped to participate in the practice itself or to interact in meaningful ways with the preacher on some kind of common ground. While the larger church community can share overall goals and expectations, the actual preparation, delivery, and evaluation of sermons can be an isolating experience that lacks interaction with others who share the training or investment in the preaching ministry of the church. Occasionally, new preachers may have a mentor in their lives; denominational structures can sometimes provide ongoing support from leaders who have experience preaching. Larger churches offer staff teams that can mentor one another in the preaching ministry. But in the vast majority of cases, pastors are isolated from the community as they prepare to preach and as they evaluate their preaching (if they evaluate their preaching at all). The idea of joint enterprise is strained when applied to preaching where the preacher is the primary or exclusive practitioner.

Therefore, some have argued that a modification of Wenger's social learning theory is needed. Geoffrey Stevenson proposes a revision of the community of practice, coining instead the term "community of agreed sermonic enterprise," proposing that preachers allow the congregation to be considered part of the joint enterprise of preaching because they do indeed play an active role as a sermon is being delivered.[15] But this refinement of Wenger's construct doesn't fully capture or leverage the value of "talking shop" with fellow practitioners who share training, expertise, or even the specific call to preach. In light of this, social learning theory challenges preaching teachers to consider the role of the congregation as a direct conversation partner in the preaching process itself, from sermon preparation through delivery to evaluation. It is worth considering whether there might be a way that we can prepare students to engage their future congregants as actual partners in the preaching endeavor and as catalysts for accelerating learning, both in the preacher and among the congregants who participate in such a joint enterprise.

In light of this challenge, teaching with trajectory should involve equipping students with a framework for creating communities of practice around themselves in the local church—ones that consist of more than just *shared repertoire* and *mutual engagement*. Social learning theory encourages teachers of preaching to conceive contexts that can provide genuine *joint enterprise* for students, equipping them to create a full community of practice around themselves for the benefit of their growth and development as preachers. Wenger draws attention to the importance of *community* in the continuing educational process, even if there remains a challenge to design it, and encourages the formation of robust communities of practice around preaching students as they head out into the local church.

---

15. Geoffrey Stevenson, "Learning to Preach: Social Learning Theory and the Development of Christian Preachers" (PhD dissertation, University of Edinburgh, 2009), 89.

Taking these two educational theories and their brief treatment above into consideration, I propose that teachers of preaching equip students with a concrete set of tools and methods for embracing the experiential learning spiral and encourage students to create a legitimate community of practice around themselves (including the dimension of joint enterprise). Teaching with this trajectory in mind does not displace the established curriculum and effective methods already in place at many institutions, nor is it impeded by the application of these same theories or other innovations to one's teaching and classrooms along the way. But teaching with trajectory advocates that preaching teachers take experiential learning theory and social learning theory into account as they add an intentionally future-oriented dimension to what they teach and how they teach it.

THE PRACTICE OF TEACHING
WITH TRAJECTORY

The role of the preaching professor is first and foremost to train up students to become accurate, relevant, and engaging preachers of the word of God. But teaching with trajectory will involve developing—even inventing—mechanisms that will keep students growing as preachers long after they graduate. Teachers of preaching can equip students with the *intentionality* of Kolb's experiential learning theory and also challenge them to embrace the *community* dimension from Wenger's social learning theory to help them formulate a future preaching context in which continuing growth can occur. These opportunities can be realized both by what preaching teachers do and what they teach.

INTENTIONALITY

Preaching teachers can encourage intentionality in students before they even leave the seminary. By casting a vision for the centrality of preaching and the importance of doing it well, they can direct students toward taking additional preaching electives while still in school to build an even stronger foundation for future ministry and learning. Many theological schools offer further training, like a ThM in Preaching, and this too can be a concrete next step for future pastors (or seasoned ones heading back to school) as they take responsibility for their own learning. Students can be encouraged to read one book on preaching each year over their first few years of ministry—a practice that may extend beyond even those early years if they discover how their own preaching can improve through exploring others' ideas about preaching. Additionally, equipping students with a version of Kolb's learning cycle specifically contextualized to preaching, and training them in its use within the weekly rhythm of preaching, can be an effective way of encouraging intentionality in the years to come. The cycle of experience, reflection, abstraction, and experimentation can become an integral part of a pastor's weekly preaching preparation.

COMMUNITY

Teachers of preaching can also encourage students to find (or develop) a preaching *community* as they prepare them for ministry. While still in seminary, students can be encouraged to be full participants in a local church. Preaching in a church is distinct from preaching in the classroom. As students build trust through faithful participation in a local church, they may get the opportunity not just to preach, but to preach to real people with whom they have formed real relationships. For some, this is facilitated by formal mentoring that is required as part of the seminary curriculum. For others, they may have to seek these relationships out on their own. But the years of seminary are sometimes mistakenly thought of as years *prior* to ministry. Instead, by investing deeply and genuinely in a local church body, ministry is already happening and growth is taking place out in the church while seminary training continues.

Students can also be encouraged to attend preaching conferences and workshops throughout their careers and to view these times together with other dedicated preachers as essential to their own continuing growth. Participation in one of the various homiletics societies is a way to become part of a larger community of practitioners who care deeply about preaching and are working to refine their craft.[16] Reading, writing, and interacting with papers can be a way of elevating one's critical engagement within the field in a way that brings one into community with others who are also pursuing excellence in preaching. Preaching teachers can encourage students to take an active role in such societies. Even though these opportunities

---

16. A good example of one such society is the Evangelical Homiletics Society (http://ehomiletics.com).

for interaction are more sporadic, they can be among the best examples of true *joint enterprise* among preachers as they endeavor to grow.

Pastors' fellowships are another context in which a preaching community can develop. Pastors can learn much from one another while at the same time having a place to talk about preaching with others who share the same call and privilege to proclaim God's word to his people. Teachers can encourage students to join one or even start one among other nearby churches in their denomination or among other churches in their area. Even where significant differences in theology or ecclesiology exist, these differences can be catalysts for significant learning if common ground is established and differences are handled respectfully and graciously.

Professors of preaching can play a role in the future ministry of students and other area pastors by creating communities of practice—even temporary ones—by providing ongoing opportunities for professional development through workshops and seminars, and through personal involvement in local churches. The teacher's influence can and should extend beyond the classroom to engage area pastors and invite them into continuing education opportunities, while casting vision for a generation of preachers who are passionate about growing and improving as ministers of the word.

There are many other ways of finding or creating communities of practice among preachers. My intent here is not to be exhaustive but rather to encourage creative thought toward the intentional development of these communities. Teaching with trajectory involves promoting these kinds of opportunities for continued learning (emphasizing intentionality and community) as essential, ongoing aspects of a healthy preaching ministry. This will help ensure that students find, or create for themselves, a continuing context for growth as they pursue lifelong learning.

INTENTIONAL COMMUNITY

One more tool has been emerging in the local church over the last few decades that weaves together the *intentionality* of Kolb's learning cycle and the *community* of Wenger's communities of practice, including the elusive aspect of *joint enterprise*. They have been called "preaching teams," "feedback groups," "creative teams," or "study groups." There is significant diversity in how they are facilitated and what they each hope to accomplish, but they are all based on a common premise: congregation members can be active participants together with the preacher in the preparation, presentation, and evaluation of the sermon. Churches have begun to experiment with collaboration in the homiletical endeavor by creating *intentional communities* focused on preaching. From an educational standpoint, collaborative homiletics offers tremendous learning potential for preachers and their congregations as they aim to grow together and increase the efficacy of the preaching ministry of the church.

COLLABORATIVE HOMILETICS

Collaborative homiletics is an approach to preaching that creates an *intentional community of practice* where preachers partner with members of their congregations to approach the preparation, delivery, and/or evaluation of sermons. In practical terms, it is a team of people from the congregation who work together with the preacher on a weekly basis to invest in the preaching ministry of the church.

This idea is not necessarily new, and in some traditions, it is even considered ancient. David Greiser, speaking out of the Anabaptist tradition, has noted that "at the heart of an Anabaptist theology of preaching is the notion that the sermon is not the work of the preacher alone but actually the project of the community of faith."[17] Nor is it a new idea that the preaching classroom "can model a congregation's participation in the sermon formation process."[18] However, implicit modeling of what might someday take place in a church setting will never be as effective as the explicit presentation of a well-developed framework for collaboration.

Any such framework needs to be based on sound educational theory as well as the practical realities of ministry in the church. Collaborative homiletics is but one example of a framework that leverages the intentionality of experiential learning and also embraces the community aspect of the social learning environment. Articulating a fully developed model for collaborative homiletics lies beyond the scope of this chapter, but there

---

17. David B. Greiser and Michael A. King, eds., *Anabaptist Preaching: A Conversation Between Pulpit, Pew, and Bible* (Telford, PA: Cascadia, 2003), 26.

18. Don M. Wardlaw, ed., *Learning Preaching: Understanding and Participating in the Process* (Lincoln, IL: The Academy of Homiletics / The Lincoln Christian College and Seminary Press, 1989), 12.

are some important applications of Kolb and Wenger that provide a foundation for effective practice.

Consider, as an example, the establishment of a preaching team that consists of a group of people within a local church who will meet weekly throughout a teaching series to work together with the preacher at this task. I present below a collaborative framework with three distinct facets of practical implementation that reflects the educational theory discussed above: bringing a team together, determining the scope of collaboration, and engaging in the collaborative homiletical endeavor.

BRINGING A TEAM TOGETHER

In most cases, the primary teaching pastor of the church should lead the initiative in bringing a team together. This protects the church's doctrine and the integrity of the homiletical process. In many churches, people can be added to the team from fellow staff members and leaders in the church. Other congregants can be included as a third category of participants, bringing a diversity of perspectives, experiences, and backgrounds to bear on the preaching task. Such a preaching team embodies Wenger's concept of *mutual engagement* if it reflects intentional diversity,[19] encouraging every member's active participation in the preaching project while still acknowledging different roles. Differences of age, gender, race, socioeconomic background, and even Christian maturity can create a healthy dynamic that improves preaching by considering the competencies and perspectives of others as any given text is preached. Preachers on the team will obviously be preparing sermons, but non-preachers cannot be mere spectators. They should be preparing by studying the text, or by thinking about potential illustrations that might help explain or prove a text, or by taking notes as a sermon is being preached to give specific and constructive feedback.

While diversity on such a team is to be valued, there must also be unity in the team's understanding of the goals and purposes of preaching. In most circumstances, the preacher is likely the only one in the room who has been through any kind of theological preparation for preaching. This may be less often the case at multi-staff churches or in churches that are

---

19. Wenger, *Communities of Practice*, 75.

near theological schools. But it cannot be assumed that a team would know the goals of preaching, the methods and mechanics of preaching, or the criteria by which preaching should be evaluated. To establish a legitimate collaborative enterprise, certain commitments should be articulated up front. Following Wenger, the next step in bringing a diverse team together is establishing a *shared repertoire* for the practice of preaching.

Wenger explains that a shared repertoire includes "routines, words, tools, ways of doing things, stories, gestures, symbols, genres, actions or concepts which the community has produced or adopted in the course of its existence, and which have become part of its practice."[20] For decades— if not centuries—churches and denominations have developed this repertoire (or set of expectations and meanings assigned to preaching) with nuances appropriate to their particular theological distinctive. These expectations need to be clearly articulated as the initial basis for successful practice. This can be as concrete as an introductory document that lays out the goals, values, community expectations, and ways of doing things that govern a local preaching ministry. It can also be helpful to generate a rubric for evaluating sermons according to this shared repertoire. A collaborative preaching team also needs clearly expressed goals and weekly expectations for participation. Developing these kinds of introductory documents together with a team can be a powerful formative experience for congregants, and clearly establishing this shared repertoire up front becomes the basis for accountability throughout the collaborative process. Preaching team participants may not have benefited from seminary training, but a well-developed shared repertoire allows every member of the team to contribute productively and successfully to the collaborative effort.

DETERMINING THE SCOPE OF COLLABORATION

Consider for the purposes of this chapter that there are three "moments" of preaching where collaboration can be applied: the preparation of a sermon, the proclamation of a sermon, and the evaluation of a sermon. Taking them in order of ease of implementation, collaboration can begin with a feedback team where, after a sermon has been delivered, it can be evaluated and feedback can be provided to the preacher. The effectiveness of such a feedback

---

20. Wenger, *Communities of Practice*, 83.

team rests on having a clearly established rubric for evaluation and some agreed-upon guidelines for providing clear feedback with kindness and grace. Some churches use "feed-forward" groups (see chapter 9) to broaden the scope of collaboration. These are groups of people who work with the preacher during the preparation moment of preaching, either as creative consultants who provide additional illustrative material or as study partners who share in the work of exegesis and sermon development.[21] Kent Walkemeyer and Tara Healy have explored a number of different possibilities for collaboration during the preparation moment of sermon development.[22] At the broadest scope of collaboration, some churches even share the proclamation moment of preaching. They invite gifted and equipped members of the congregation to preach, working together with the pastor and the preaching team in the preparation and evaluation of their sermon. There is no single correct implementation of collaboration; each church should be able to determine a scope of collaboration that makes sense based on its own culture and theological commitments.

These options for collaboration can be envisioned as a matrix with the various participants along one axis and the various moments of preaching along the other, as represented in figure 10.3.

	preparation	delivery	evaluation
pastoral staff			
leadership			
laity			

FIGURE 10.3. The Matrix of Collaboration for Preaching Teams

21. Ken Shigematsu, "Hitting Your Creative Peak," *PreachingToday.com*, June 2015, http://www.preachingtoday.com/skills/2015/june/hitting-your-creative-peak.html.

22. Kent Walkemeyer and Tara Healy, "Evaluating Collaborative Approaches to Preparing and Delivering Sermons" (paper presented at the annual conference for the Evangelical Homiletics Society, La Mirada, CA, October 11–13, 2007). In this paper, the authors identify five variations on the idea of sermon preparation teams: mapping, creating, studying, assisting, and coaching.

Some churches can operate with a comprehensive scope of collaboration, essentially putting a checkmark in every box in the above chart by involving pastoral staff, leadership, and laity all working together as a team on the preparation, delivery, and evaluation of sermons. Pastors may do the majority of preaching, but there can be room for gifted and equipped laypeople to participate as preachers on the team if deemed appropriate or desirable based on the church's view of the pulpit. In other churches, however, for theological or practical reasons, it is not possible to effectively implement such extensive collaboration. It may be more appropriate to start with something less involved, like creating a sermon feedback group. Whether it is for a single sermon, for a teaching series, or for a full season of life in the church, any expression within this scope of collaboration can become the seed for establishing a true community of practice, where preachers can intentionally leverage the weekly rhythm of preaching as an opportunity to continue learning.

Once the team is formed, however, the members still need concrete guidance to make the best use of their time together. Completing Wenger's community of practice, the team enters into the weekly rhythm of sermon preparation, delivery, and evaluation together, providing a legitimate context for *joint enterprise.*

THE COLLABORATIVE HOMILETICAL ENDEAVOR

The weekly rhythm of preaching is well suited to establishing *joint enterprise* by applying Kolb's experiential learning cycle to the collaborative effort.

Begin with a sermon that has just been preached. As the preaching team meets later that week, the team will evaluate the sermon based on the agreed-upon rubric and the commitments to preaching discussed earlier. This evaluation corresponds to the *reflective observation* phase of Kolb's cycle, as team participants interact with one another and with the preacher to celebrate the effectiveness of the sermon and to identify some suggestions for improvement. Receiving feedback is a challenging, vulnerable experience for a preacher, so it is worth establishing a safe environment for this kind of evaluation. This safe environment is also necessary because disagreement can take place between the preacher and the other team members or even between fellow participants. However, Wenger acknowledges and even celebrates such disagreement as having significant inherent learning potential if handled well.[23]

Feedback, however, does not automatically generate learning in the preacher. It needs to be processed through the second stage of the experiential learning cycle, *abstract conceptualization*. The team, or the preacher, needs to take that feedback and work it into suggestions, cautions, or principles that can be applied to a new text and a new sermon. Without this work of developing transferrable principles, much of the learning from the feedback is lost by the time the next sermon comes along.

The third stage in the learning cycle involves *active experimentation*, wherein the preacher applies that which they have learned to a new sermon. Preachers do not need to apply everything they learned from one week into their next sermon; the educational value of the reflection and conceptualization stages accumulates from week to week, and the preacher has the freedom to intentionally experiment with any upcoming sermon. If the team is working together in the preparation of sermons, there can be conversation about how previous learning is being applied. In such a model, a preacher might propose the sermon's big idea, along with a sermon's structure, main ideas, and illustrative material. The team's involvement in this developmental stage of sermon preparation allows the preacher to learn from the study, insights, experiences, and encouragement (or if necessary, correction and reproof) of the team before a sermon is preached.

Concrete experience closes the cycle as a sermon is preached. The skill of preaching is actually practiced as the word of God is proclaimed to his people. This, then, triggers another round of the experiential learning cycle, capturing the educational potential of the entire collaborative homiletical endeavor.

The preacher isn't the only one who learns and grows through this collaboration. With multiple passes through this cycle, the members of the preaching team also grow in their understanding of preaching, their understanding of God's word, and their commitment to the preaching ministry of the church. A genuine community of practice develops, one that involves legitimate *joint enterprise* among a group of people who are

---

23. Wenger, *Communities of Practice*, 78.

growing together in the skill of preaching and who are able to engage in the preaching ministry of the church in genuinely significant ways. As different people from the congregation experience this collaborative experience, biblical literacy is promoted throughout the church, grounded exegetical methodology is shared among those who may be leading Bible studies in other church ministries, and deep relationships can form that can help prevent the sense of isolation that pastors often feel when they find themselves alone in their studies. A collaborative approach to the preaching ministry of the church blesses both the preacher and the church, cementing a real partnership as the entire community pursues God's mission together. The preacher no longer experiences mere incidental or accidental growth; the preacher is positioned to engage in active, purposeful learning within the *intentional community* of a preaching team.

COLLABORATIVE HOMILETICS AND TEACHING WITH TRAJECTORY

The above discussion of collaborative homiletics and educational theory is not intended to be a comprehensive manual or a complete presentation of the range of possible approaches. Instead, it is intended to stimulate thinking about collaborative frameworks that could be taught as part of the seminary preaching curriculum. The goal is to equip students with tools they can implement in the local church that will enable them to capture the educational potential of those early years of a new preaching ministry. With some careful thought, and building on educational theory, teachers of preaching can cast a vision for lifelong learning and provide a framework for accomplishing it. Because of the variety of possible approaches to collaboration, it may be up to individual professors to develop their own set of recommended practices for a collaborative homiletical method.

Most teachers of preaching are already employing a collaborative framework at the seminary level in some form or another. Students can often be found working together to identify the central idea from a given text or preaching to one another and receiving feedback from their peers and teacher. Teachers recognize its efficacy in helping students learn to preach. Developing and teaching a collaborative homiletical framework for use in the local church is just one way to teach with trajectory and prepare students to keep growing as preachers throughout the many years of ministry that lay ahead. In addition to being well trained at the seminary level, students will also become able champions of their own continuing education.

CONCLUSION

Whether it's using a collaborative framework or equipping students with some other tools for the task, it is the preaching teacher's responsibility to do more than provide the foundation for a student's future preaching ministry. Your greatest hope is that your students will continue to learn and develop as preachers throughout their lives. The challenge is moving students beyond the basic piano scales and introductory theory to become masters whose hands fly across the keys with beauty and grace, able to communicate through the music of preaching the great unsearchable wisdom of the living God that he has chosen to reveal by his Spirit and through his word.

As a teacher of preaching, you are only part of your students' journey; their best learning is yet to come, if you can equip them to capture it.

o o o

Postscript: You Are an Educator

*The more that I taught, the more I was convinced that
the best method of teaching was a healthy rhythm
of teaching, practice, and evaluation—combined
with observation of experienced preachers.*[24]

This book has moved from a survey of the preaching professor's key role in the United States to the strategic elements a newly minted preaching professor needs to know to begin teaching homiletics. Hopefully, after reading the chapters and practicing what you have read in your preparation for teaching, you are better equipped to tackle the classroom and help your students to preach well. As one preaching professor observed, "The goal for beginning preachers should be to become competent, not excellent."

As this book concludes, let me encourage you to continue growing. There is much more to learn. For example, the integration of various subject areas in preaching is a constant challenge for the students and for the teacher. Students tend to be siloed in their coursework. They may have just completed a course in church history or even exegesis but fail to build bridges of integration into the task of preaching. This is an area where the skilled professor of homiletics will require continued education. "I wish I had known that so few students begin their homiletical studies with good exegetical skills—or worse, without seeing the need for them," mourns one professor. He continues, "Of those who've completed coursework in hermeneutics, only a small percentage have taken time to think through

---

24. Anonymous preaching professor from the survey for this book.

how they should apply what they learned in those courses to the task of preaching."

Another area this book did not address concerns multicultural matters in preaching and in teaching. One insightful professor reflected:

> I wish I knew that the preaching of Europe and North America does not define biblical communication. The preachers in Scripture preached very differently. They tailored their sermons so that God's message fit with the culture and situation of their audiences. In preaching, one size (or sermon form) does not fit all, and we fail our students when we fail to point this out.

Still another professor thoughtfully wrote, "I wish I had enjoyed the opportunity of sitting under teachers of preaching whose cultural backgrounds differed from my own. I could have then carried that broader view of our craft into the classroom starting on day one."

Similarly, one preaching professor raised the issue of the multilayered texture of North American culture and subcultures. He commented:

> I wish I would have been more aware of how much both the larger culture of North America and the church-world sub-culture of North America influence the importance of preaching, the stated and unstated value of preaching, and the forms/methods of preaching. Specifically, megachurch pastors have *huge* platforms and much greater influence over homiletics than do seminaries. This is a continual challenge, especially when some of the methods being modeled are less than helpful to students. Moreover, the dominance of media/technology in its current iterations was unforeseen twenty to twenty-five years ago and requires constant interaction. Finally, as evangelicalism has continued to evolve and become ever more diverse, preaching is not nearly as valued in many of its quarters as was true thirty-five years ago.

Although this book does not address matters of integrating learning across disciplines of study or learning from a variety of cultures and subcultures, or other important issues that intersect with preaching, the basics for starting out are in these pages. In this book you have received a good grounding in homiletics andragogy, but educators always continue to cultivate learning in themselves and in their students.

You are an educator. Continue to learn.

o   o   o

Appendix 1: Sermon Grading Rubric

Name:_____ Intended Listeners:_____
Text:_____ Grade:_____

STATEMENT OF THE CENTRAL IDEA

What is the sermon's central idea?

How well was it communicated? (Circle one)

   1   2   3   4   5   6   7   8   9   10

BIBLICAL ACCURACY

Was the text clearly communicated?

Was this sermon genre sensitive by matching the style of the biblical genre? (Circle one)

Not at all   Seldom   Occasionally   Absolutely

How well was the sermon's content anchored in the text? (Circle one)

   1   2   3   4   5   6   7   8   9   10

STRUCTURE

Was the introduction effective in gaining attention, surfacing needs, building tension, and orienting to the rest of the sermon? Did you want to continue listening? (Circle one)

Poor   Mediocre   Interesting   Outstanding

Was the sermon clear and easy to follow? Did the transitions help the sermon have unity and progress? How?

How would you rate the structure? (Circle one)

1   2   3   4   5   6   7   8   9   10

DELIVERY

How were the preacher's gestures, expressions, eye contact, vocal dynamics, and tone?

How would you rate the delivery? (Circle one)

1   2   3   4   5   6   7   8   9   10

APPLICATION/CONCLUSION

What illustrations or examples were used, and how did they impact the message? What questions do you think listeners still have? Was the sermon engaging?

Was there a clear summary? Was there an effective call to action and envisioning hope for the future?

Did this sermon fit this particular audience/occasion, and how do you think listeners will respond after hearing it?

How would you rate the application/conclusion? (Circle one)

1   2   3   4   5   6   7   8   9   10

○ ○ ○

Appendix 2: Sermon Rubric Explained

STATEMENT OF THE CENTRAL IDEA

- 1–3. The student did not state a clear central idea for the passage.

- 4–6. The student attempted to state a central idea, but it was unclear or only partial (i.e., subject/complement only).

- 7–8. The student clearly stated a central idea in subject and complement form, but it was not memorable.

- 9–10. The student clearly stated a central idea in subject and complement form that was memorable and accurate.

BIBLICAL ACCURACY

- 1–3. The student did not explicitly refer to the passage.

- 4–6. The student referred to the passage but did not read the relevant portion of the text or make appropriate exegetical observations from the passage itself.

- 7–8. The student anchored the content of the sermon to the text by reading the relevant portion of the text but did not make appropriate exegetical observations from the passage.

- 9–10. The student explained the text, anchored the content of the sermon to the passage by reading the relevant portion of the text, and made appropriate exegetical observations.

STRUCTURE

- 1–3. The student did not organize the content of the sermon into movements that were logical, clearly stated, and connected by smooth transitions.

- 4–6. The student organized the content of the sermon into movements, but they were not logical, and the transitions did not show the relationship between each point of the sermon.

- 7–8. The student organized the content of the sermon into movements that were logical and clearly stated but did not use transitions to show the relationship to major movements of the sermon.

- 9–10. The student organized the content of the sermon into movements that were logical, clearly stated, and connected by smooth transitions that showed the logical relationship between movements.

DELIVERY

- 1–3. The student did not vary volume and pitch or use meaningful gestures.

- 4–6. The student used some gestures but they were not meaningful and the use of vocal variety was distracting.

- 7–8. The student spoke with variety in volume and pitch and used appropriate gestures, but not consistently.

- 9–10. The student spoke with variety in both volume and pitch and used meaningful gestures that were appropriate to the content and flow of the sermon throughout the message.

APPLICATION/CONCLUSION

- 1–3. The student did not apply the text to the audience, and the sermon lacked any application to life.

- 4–6. The student applied the text to the audience, but the applications were not consistent with the text or did not include examples and principles for life and faith.

- 7–8. The student applied the text to the audience by stating principles that were clearly consistent with the text and gave concrete examples, but they were superficial or trite.

- 9–10. The student applied the text to the audience by stating principles that were clearly consistent with the text and gave concrete examples of what the principles look like in real life situations, envisioning hope for the future.

Contributors

Victor D. Anderson (PhD, Biola University) is professor of pastoral ministries at Dallas Theological Seminary, Dallas, TX.

Patricia M. Batten (DMin, Gordon-Conwell Theological Seminary) is ranked adjunct assistant professor of preaching at Gordon-Conwell Theological Seminary, South Hamilton, MA.

Timothy Bushfield (MDiv, Gordon-Conwell Theological Seminary; PhD candidate, London School of Theology/Middlesex University, in association with the A. J. Gordon Guild of Gordon-Conwell Theological Seminary, South Hamilton, MA) is lead pastor, Community Church of East Gloucester, Gloucester, MA.

Sid Buzzell (PhD, University of Michigan) is professor of biblical exposition (retired), Colorado Christian University, Lakewood, CO.

Scott M. Gibson (DPhil, University of Oxford) holds the David E. Garland Chair of Preaching and is the director of the PhD in Preaching Program at Baylor University/Truett Seminary, Waco, TX. He is cofounder of the Evangelical Homiletics Society and the author or coauthor of several books on preaching.

Tony Merida (PhD, New Orleans Baptist Theological Seminary) is pastor for preaching and vision at Imago Dei Church in Raleigh, NC.

Blake Newsom (PhD, New Orleans Baptist Theological Seminary) is dean of the chapel and assistant professor of expository preaching at New Orleans Baptist Theological Seminary, New Orleans, LA and senior pastor of Dauphin Way Baptist Church, Mobile, AL.

Chris Rappazini (ThM, University of Edinburgh; PhD candidate, Gonzaga University) is assistant professor of applied theology and church ministries at Moody Bible Institute, Chicago, IL.

John V. Tornfelt (EdD, Trinity Evangelical Divinity School) is professor of preaching and ministry (retired) at Evangelical Theological Seminary, Myerstown, PA.

○ ○ ○

Name and Subject Index

written, 160
See also learning level; syllabus
feelers, 65–66
See also learning styles; Myers-
   Briggs Type Indicator;
   personality
Felder, Richard, 63
figure
   3.1, 42
   3.2, 44
   4.1, 63
   4.2, 67
   4.3, 68
   10.1, 171
   10.2, 174
   10.3, 183
First Baptist Church, Haverhill, MA,
   18n50
Fitch, Eleazar T., 8
Freire, Paulo, 38n3, 39n7, 47, 48, 56n25

G

Gambrell, Mary, 13
Garrett Theological Seminary, 9
George W. Truett Theological
   Seminary, 9
Gibson, Scott M., 24, 151n4, 153
Giroux, Henry, 48, 56n25
goals
   achievable, 29
   learning intentions, and, 133–34,
      138–39, 141, 147
      See also learning intentions
   motivation, and, 32–33
   performance-approach, 31
   teaching, 77–80, 128
   work-avoidant, 31
Goodrich, Chauncey A., 8
Gordon-Conwell Theological
   Seminary, 15n43, 77, 151n4, 153
Gordon Divinity School, 9
Grace Baptist Church in Philadelphia,
   14
Grace Theological Seminary, 151n4

grading
   ethics of, 132
   scale, 119–20
   sermon grading rubric, 66, 155
   student motivation, and, 154
   students challenge your, when,
      160–61
   syllabi and, 112–14, 123–25
   various roles of, 154
   See also assessment; learning level;
      syllabus
grammatical diagramming, 103
   See also sermon development; study
Grasha, Anthony, 71
Grasha and Riechmann-Hruska's
   Student Learning Styles, 71
   See also learning styles; social
      interaction
Gregorc, Anthony, 68
Gregorc's Style Delineator Approach,
   68–69
   See also information processing;
      learning styles
Greidanus, Sidney, 152
Greiser, David, 180
*Grit: The Power and Passion of
   Perseverance* (Duckworth), 28
   See also Duckworth, Angela

H

Haddon W. Robinson Center for
   Preaching, 15n43
Hannah, John D., 9n18
Hart, Levi, 13
Harvard
   College, 6, 12, 15
   Divinity School, 7–8
Hawking, Stephen, 130
Healy, Tara, 183
Henson, Kenneth, 74
hermeneutics,
   Christocentric, 81
   exegesis and, 56, 70, 125
   field of, 80, 103

o   o   o

Scripture Index